At Issue

Organ Transplants

Other Books in the At Issue Series:

At Issue

| Organ Transplants

Diane Andrews Henningfeld, Book Editor

GREENHAVEN PRESS
A part of Gale, Cengage Learning

GALE
CENGAGE Learning·

Detroit • New York • San Francisco • New Haven, Conn • Waterville, Maine • London

GALE
CENGAGE Learning·

Elizabeth Des Chenes, *Managing Editor*

© 2012 Greenhaven Press, a part of Gale, Cengage Learning.

Gale and Greenhaven Press are registered trademarks used herein under license.

For more information, contact:
Greenhaven Press
27500 Drake Rd.
Farmington Hills, MI 48331-3535
Or you can visit our Internet site at http://www.gale.cengage.com

For product information and technology assistance, contact us at

Gale Customer Support, 1-800-877-4253
For permission to use material from this text or product, submit all requests online at www.cengage.com/permissions

Further permissions questions can be emailed to permissionrequest@cengage.com

Articles in Greenhaven Press anthologies are often edited for length to meet page requirements. In addition, original titles of these works are changed to clearly present the main thesis and to explicitly indicate the author's opinion. Every effort is made to ensure that Greenhaven Press accurately reflects the original intent of the authors. Every effort has been made to trace the owners of copyrighted material.

Cover Image copyright, Debra Hughes, 2007. Used under license from Shutterstock.com.

LIBRARY OF CONGRESS CATALOGING-IN-PUBLICATION DATA

Organ transplants / Diane Andrews Henningfeld, book editor.
    p. cm. -- (At issue)
    Includes bibliographical references and index.
    ISBN 978-0-7377-5586-2 (hardcover) -- ISBN 978-0-7377-5587-9 (pbk.)
    1. Transplantation of organs, tissues, etc. 2. Transplantation of organs, tissues, etc.--Moral and ethical aspects. I. Henningfeld, Diane Andrews. II. Title. III. Series.
    RD120.7.O735 2012
    617.9'54--dc23
                                          2011048273

Printed in the United States of America
2 3 4 5 6   18 17 16 15 14

Contents

Introduction

The first successful organ transplant was a kidney transplant performed in 1954, according to the United Network for Organ Sharing (UNOS). In the decades that followed, doctors began developing ways to transplant other organs. However, the difficult problem of organ rejection by patient immune systems prevented organ transplants from becoming widespread. The first immunosuppressant drugs used to prevent organ rejection also "killed the patient's bone marrow," according to Kimberly G. Baskette and John M. Ritz in the *Technology Teacher* in 2010. Without bone marrow, patients were vulnerable to infections and often died. However, during the 1970s, the well-tolerated and highly effective immunosuppressive drug cyclosporine was developed, opening the door to more and more organ transplants.

But the use of cyclosporine led to another seemingly intractable problem: organ shortages. With organ transplant survivorship increasing, and with the growing number of organs that could be transplanted successfully, the demand for human organs for transplantation grew exponentially. By September 2011, the number of people in the United States waiting for organs for transplantation grew to more than 112,000, up from 104,296 in 2009, according to UNOS statistics. Many of these people die while on the waiting list, simply because organs are not available. Baskette and Ritz note that only 27 percent of people who need transplants receive them.

Some organs can be procured from living donors. For example, because normally each person has two kidneys, one kidney can be given to another person with minimal consequences for the donor. However, most organs, such as hearts and lungs, can only be procured from people who have died. In addition, those organs must be harvested immediately upon the declaration of death in order for them to be of sufficient quality for transplantation. In the US, unless a person is a registered organ donor, or has made his or her wishes known to family members, the organs cannot be removed. Thus, many potentially useful organs are buried or cremated with the body.

Scott Carney, in *Wired* on May 8, 2007, reports that a 2005 Gallup Poll revealed that more than half of all Americans would offer up their organs for donation after death. Other studies place that figure as high as 90 percent. Yet, according to Carney, less than 20 percent of families choose organ donation for relatives who have died. The statistic reveals a fact at the center of the organ shortage: far more people want to donate organs than actually register to be organ donors. Although many education programs designed to increase organ donor registration have been launched, the percentage of registered donors has not budged. Organ shortages continue unabated and promise to grow.

Presumed consent, a plan that advocates assert has the potential to solve the problem, is already in place in many European countries such as France, Austria, Italy, Denmark, and Spain. In places where presumed consent has been legislated, if a person dies without having made an explicit objection to having his or her organs used for transplantation, it is presumed that the person consents to having his or her organs used in this way. Presumed consent is considered an "opt-out" process, as contrasted with the "opt-in" process currently in place in the United States. In the US, people must register on their drivers' licenses or through other means, to opt-in for organ donation. According to the Presumed Consent Foundation, in countries with presumed consent legislation, only about 2 percent opt out of the program.

Scholars Alberto Abadie and Sebastien Gay, in a 2006 article in the *Journal of Health Economics*, write that in countries enacting presumed consent legislation, such legislation "has a positive and sizeable effect on organ donation rates." In the

United Kingdom, which is considering presumed consent legislation, studies show consistently that donation rates could be increased by 25 to 30 percent. (Scholars are also quick to caution, however, that even this large of an increase in donations would not fully alleviate the organ shortage in the United States.)

Several state legislatures in the US have proposed enacting presumed consent legislation. In January 2011, Colorado began such a debate. While many transplant activists are working hard for the passage of laws permitting presumed consent, not all citizens approve of or support an opt-out system. Hastings Center fellow Mary Ann Baily, in the *New York Times* on May 2, 2010, comments on legislation introduced in the New York State Assembly to enact presumed consent:

> What on earth leads the assemblyman to think that the public will accept presumed consent? ... Some already fear that signing a donor card may make physicians give up on them too soon, especially if the hospital is likely to lose money on their care. This legislation, if enacted, might only ratchet up those fears.

Some critics of presumed consent argue that such a system will so alienate the public that organ donations will actually go down.

Nevertheless, until the US devises an effective way to increase organ donation, whether through presumed consent, increased education of the public, or changing definitions of what constitutes death, the organ shortage will continue to be the single most difficult issue in organ transplantation.

The authors of the following viewpoints examine the organ shortage and potential strategies that could increase the number of organs available for transplant. They also consider such controversial topics as transplant tourism, organ allocation, illegal organ trafficking, and payment for human organs. Indeed, the following viewpoints demonstrate that organ transplantation is not merely a topic for medical workers. It is a complex ethical, political, and social issue that should be addressed by an informed public able to make good decisions about life—and death.

1

Organ Transplants: An Overview

Arthur Caplan

Arthur Caplan chairs the department of medical ethics at the University of Pennsylvania.

With over 100,000 people in the United States on the waiting list for donated organs, many hard choices must be made concerning what criteria should be used for organ distribution. One option for increasing organ supply is to establish an organ market, though most people believe this is unethical. A presumed consent system wherein it is presumed that someone wants to be a donor unless he or she specifically opts out is another solution, though some believe this is a violation of the donor's rights.

Every day about a dozen people in the United States die waiting for organ transplants. The deaths are especially tragic since many might be prevented if more organs were available. Every day very hard choices have to be made about who will live and who will die. With close to 100,000 people on waiting lists for kidneys, hearts, livers, lungs, and intestines, the pressure to distribute scarce organs fairly and to find ways to increase their supply is enormous.

Growing Waiting Lists

The pressure is getting worse because waiting lists are growing faster than the supply of organs. And if transplant centers were to relax their standards to include more people—such as

Arthur Caplan, "Organ Transplantation," *The Hasting Center Bioethics Briefing Book for Journalists, Policymakers, and Campaigns*, ed. Mary Crowley, Garrison, NY: The Hasting Center, 2008, pp. 120–32. Copyright © 2008 by the Hastings Center. All rights reserved. Reproduced by permission.

those who lack insurance, have severe intellectual disabilities, older persons, prisoners, illegal aliens, and foreigners who cannot get transplants in their own countries—then the lists of those waiting could easily triple or quadruple.

To close this gap, policymakers will have to consider new options for inducing people to donate organs, and organ transplant centers may have to rethink their criteria for determining who is allowed on their waiting lists and who has priority. These decisions involve many ethical and legal issues, including:

- Who on the waiting lists should get transplants first: patients in the greatest need or those most likely to benefit?

- Should certain people, like illegal aliens, foreigners, and people with a history of addiction or a criminal record, be denied a place on waiting lists?

- Should people be paid to donate their organs?

- Should federal law be changed to permit people to buy and sell organs?

Distributing Organs: What Is Just and Fair?

Rationing is unavoidable in organ transplantation, but the system for allocating organs must be just and fair. Justice requires some rule or policy that insures that the supply of donated organs is used wisely and consistently with what donors and their families would wish, such as giving priority to saving children's lives, or to American citizens. Fairness demands that like cases be treated alike and that the allocation system be transparent, so that all who wait know why some are selected and some are not.

There are valid questions about the justice and fairness of the current system. Transplant centers are the gatekeepers who decide whom they will and will not admit as transplant candidates. Their policies vary. Many nonmedical values shape their decisions, and it can be argued that some centers invoke these values in ways that are not truly just. Among these considerations:

- Many transplant centers will not accept people without insurance.

- Transplant teams rarely consider anyone over 75 years of age.

- Some centers exclude patients with moderate mental retardation, HIV, a history of addiction, or a long criminal record.

- Though American transplant centers can list foreigners, they can make up no more than 5% of any center's list. Most of non-U.S. citizens listed have substantial financial resources and pay in cash.

- Some transplant programs will admit illegal aliens, but most are children. Some transplant centers have caused controversy by refusing to retransplant illegal aliens whose initial organs, received at the same hospital during childhood, have failed.

The Role of Value Judgments

Value judgments may also influence the process of matching cadaver organs with patients on the waiting lists. The United Network for Organ Sharing (UNOS), a national network based in Richmond, Virginia, bears this responsibility. At present, its driving considerations are matching a donor and a recipient by blood type, tissue type, and organ size. Some weight is also given to the urgency or need for a transplant as reflected by time on the waiting list and the person's physical condition. There has been some push in recent years to steer organs toward those who are not seriously ill so as to maximize the chances for successful transplantation. UNOS used to have to allocate organs locally, but recently it has moved to a more regional distribution, as organ preservation techniques and other aspects of organ transplantation have improved.

Debates are growing louder about the criteria that should be used to dominate UNOS's distribution process—should it be the urgency of a patient's medical need? Or should it be efficacy? In recent years, there has been a shift toward efficacy. UNOS proposed new regulations, available to the public on its Web site, in an effort to improve the fairness of the allocation process.

Furthermore, patients can increase their chances of getting a transplant by enrolling at more then one transplant center—a practice known as multiple listing. About 10% of the current waiting list consists of persons who are listed at more than one center. Critics of multiple listing say that it is unjust because it gives an advantage to people with the resources to pay for more than one evaluation and listing. Each evaluation can cost tens of thousands of dollars.

Increasing the Supply

A number of steps have been taken over the years to try to increase the supply of organs. The first attempt was from state laws permitting the use of organ donor cards or family consent to donate a deceased relative's organs. Then, states began requiring hospitals to ask all patients' families about organ donation. Most recently, state laws required hospitals to honor a patient's donor card even when the family opposed donation.

None of these policies has significantly increased the supply of organs. Therefore, some people now argue for a shift away from a reliance on voluntary altruism in organ donation toward either a paid market or presumed consent.

Organ Markets Raise Ethical Concerns

Two basic strategies have been proposed to provide incentives for people to sell their organs upon their death. One strategy is simply to permit organ sale by changing the National Organ Transplant Act (NOTA), the federal law that bans organ sales. Then, individuals would be free to broker contracts with persons interested in selling at prices mutually agreed upon by both parties. Markets already exist on the Internet between potential live donors and people in need of organs, but these transactions are illegal. The other strategy is a regulated market in which the government would act as the purchaser of organs—setting a fixed price and enforcing conditions of sale. Both proposals have drawn heated ethical criticism.

Selling organs, even in a tightly regulated market, violates the ethics of medicine.

One criticism is that only the poor and desperate will want to sell their body parts. If you need money, you might sell your kidney to try and feed your family or to pay back a debt. This may be a "rational" decision, but that does not make it a matter of free choice. Watching your child go hungry when you have no job and a wealthy person waves a wad of bills in your face is not exactly a scenario that inspires confidence in the fairness of a market for body parts. Talk of individual rights and autonomy is hollow if those with no options must "choose" to sell their organs to purchase life's necessities. Choice requires information, options, and some degree of freedom, as well as the ability to reason.

It is hard to imagine many people in wealthy countries eager to sell their organs upon their death. In fact, even if compensation is relatively high, few will agree to sell. That has been the experience with markets in human eggs for research purposes and with paid surrogacy in the United States—prices have escalated, but there are still relatively few sellers. Selling organs, even in a tightly regulated market, violates the ethics of medicine. The core ethical norm of the medical profession is the principle, "Do no harm." The only way that removing an organ from someone seems morally defensible is if the donor chooses to undergo the harm of surgery solely to help another, and if there is sufficient medical benefit to the recipient.

The main ethical objection to presumed consent is the perceived loss of patient autonomy—that it is wrong to take someone's organs without that person's explicit consent.

The creation of a market puts medicine in the position of removing body parts from people solely to abet those people's interest in securing compensation. A market in human organs has a model in the existing market for human eggs for assisted reproduction and research purposes, but that practice is highly controversial. Is this a role that the health professions can ethically countenance? In a market—even a regulated one—doctors and nurses still would be using their skills to help people harm themselves solely for money. The resulting distrust and loss of professional standards is too a high price to pay to gamble on the hope that a market may secure more organs for those in need.

Increasing Donations Through Presumed Consent

There is another option for increasing the organ supply that has not been tried in the United States but is practiced abroad. Spain, Italy, Austria, Belgium, and some other European countries have enacted laws that create presumed consent, or what I prefer to call "default to donation." In such a system, the presumption is that you want to be an organ donor upon your death—the default to donation. People who don't want to be organ donors have to say so by registering this wish on a computer, carrying a card, or telling their loved ones. With default to donation, no one's rights are taken away—voluntary altruism remains the moral foundation for making organs available, and, therefore, procuring organs is consistent with medical ethics. Based on the European experience, there is a good chance America could get a significant jump in the supply of organs by shifting to a default-to-donation policy. Donation rates in European countries with presumed consent are about 25% higher than in other European nations.

Default to donation proposals have been submitted in several states. The United Kingdom is also considering implementing presumed consent, and if it does—and if the policy is successful—that may provide more momentum for trying it in the United States. The main ethical objection to presumed consent is the perceived loss of patient autonomy—that it is wrong to take someone's organs without that person's explicit consent. In addition, some people believe that presumed consent violates the 5th Amendment prohibition against taking private property without due process and compensation. Critics are also concerned about mistakes in which there is the presumption that someone consented when, in fact, either the individual had failed to indicate opposition or the record of that opposition was lost.

On the Horizon

The need for organ transplantation may eventually be reduced by stem cell therapies. Scientists hope to repair or even replace damaged organs with new cells grown from adult or embryonic stem cells. Earlier this year, researchers at the University of Minnesota reported that they had built a beating heart in a laboratory with stem cells from neonatal and fetal rats. And British scientists are undertaking pioneering clinical trials that attempt to repair the hearts of heart attack patients by injecting them with stem cells.

2

The US Has Failed to Establish an Effective Organ Procurement Policy

T. Randolph Beard, John D. Jackson, and David L. Kaserman

T. Randolph Beard, John D. Jackson, and David L. Kaserman are professors of economics at Auburn University.

Around the world, there is an ongoing and severe shortage of organs available for transplantation. Improvements in technology and immunosuppressive drugs have made organ transplants safer and more practical, exacerbating the shortages. Public policies for meeting the demand, including educational efforts, organ donor cards, requiring doctors to request organ donations, kidney exchanges, and reimbursement of donor costs, have remained largely ineffective. The only effective solution to the organ shortage is to financially reward the families of potential organ donors for the donation of a deceased family member's organs.

As anyone even vaguely familiar with the organ transplantation industry is keenly aware, there is a severe and long-standing shortage of human organs made available for transplant in both the United States and abroad. Every year for at least the last 30 years, the number of patients in need of organ transplants—primarily kidneys, hearts, livers, and lungs—has exceeded the number of deceased organ donors by a considerable margin. As a result, transplant waiting lists have continued to expand . . . and expected waiting times have

T. Randolph Beard, John D. Jackson, and David L. Kaserman, "The Failure of U.S. Organ Procurement Policy," *Regulation*, Winter 2008, pp. 22–30. Copyright © 2008 by CATO Institute. All rights reserved. Reproduced by permission.

grown apace. The principal (and predictable) upshot of the ongoing shortage is an increasing number of deaths of patients who, because of an insufficient supply of deceased donors, fail to receive the needed organs in time.

As a direct consequence of . . . technological constraint, there were no transplant waiting lists and no obvious organ shortage in the late 1950s and early 1960s.

Meanwhile, transplant professionals and academic observers have been engaged in a prolonged and often heated debate regarding potential policy actions that might be adopted to resolve the shortage. There has been a series of largely ineffective policy responses ranging from increased educational spending, to donor cards, to the latest strategy involving diffusion of so-called "best practice" procurement techniques. Notably absent from this parade of remedies is the one policy that is likely to end the organ shortage: the adoption of financial incentives for cadaveric organ donors.

While proposals for the use of such incentives have been advanced for almost as long as the shortage has existed, opposition to this option has remained both highly vocal and adamant. Such opposition is ostensibly based upon a set of ethical concerns, although no one has yet articulated a sensible, ethical reason for why we should continue to allow thousands of patients to die each year instead of paying surviving families a few thousand dollars to motivate an increased rate of consent for organ removal.

The Organ Shortage

The first successful human organ transplant in the United States was performed on December 23, 1954. On that date, a kidney was transplanted from a living donor who was an identical twin of the recipient. The body's immune system will attack what it perceives to be a foreign organism and, in the early days of organ transplantation, there were no advanced immunosuppressive drugs that would prevent the rejection of "foreign" organs. As a result, the only organ for which transplantation was feasible was the kidney and the only donors who were technologically suitable were living, closely related biological relatives of the recipient. As a direct consequence of that technological constraint, there were no transplant waiting lists and no obvious organ shortage in the late 1950s and early 1960s. In effect, organ transplant candidates brought the necessary donor with them when they checked into the hospital for the transplant operation. If there was no acceptable (and willing) donor, no transplant could be performed.

Importantly, given the constraints, there was no obvious need for either an independent organ procurement agency or any explicit payment to motivate donor cooperation. The transplant candidates themselves or their families were responsible for locating donors. The close personal affection between the donor and recipient was generally thought to be sufficient to motivate the donor to supply the needed organ. Where it was not sufficient, additional motivation could be provided by emotional pressure, direct (but clandestine) payments, or both.

Those intra-family arrangements remained largely out of sight of the transplant centers and physicians. Consequently, a system of so-called "altruistic" supply seemed to make sense, and reliance on such a system initially did not seriously impede the use of the emerging medical technology.

Technology Creates Greater Demand

This situation changed as transplant technology began to advance. Improvements were made gradually in both surgical techniques and immunosuppressive pharmaceuticals. It is difficult to pinpoint precisely when organ shortages first appeared because of the absence of the earlier data. Projecting backward from more recent figures and surveying the prior literature, however, it appears that transplant patient waiting lists probably began to form in the early to mid 1970s.

The growth of these lists was accelerated greatly by the introduction of the first modern immunosuppressive drug, cyclosporine, which was adopted in the United States in 1983. Its introduction, along with a series of subsequent pharmaceutical discoveries, had two important impacts on the transplant industry. First, because of the improved ability to suppress the transplant recipient's immune system, graft survival rates increased dramatically as rejection problems began to be brought under control. Rising success rates, in turn, stimulated transplant demand as patients faced improved prospects for an effective cure. Second and importantly, as a direct consequence of the new drugs, it became increasingly feasible to employ organs from deceased (and anonymous to recipients) donors. This development allowed transplant technology to be expanded to vital organs other than kidneys. Thus, patients suffering heart, liver, or lung failure were presented new hope as cadaveric organs began to be transplanted successfully.

This technologically driven expansion from living to deceased donors, along with rising success rates, broke the prior necessity of a biological relationship between the organ donor and the recipient. As a result, patients were no longer responsible for locating their own donors. Waiting lists began to expand as the number of potential transplant recipients rapidly grew.

Initially, the queues and the early attempts to collect organs from deceased donors' families were managed by the organ transplant centers that also performed the surgical operations. Given their now two-decade experience with the altruistic system, the centers' organ procurement activities continued to rely solely upon the zero-price policy that seemed to have performed well in the past. Thus, a procurement policy inherited from the earlier period of living, related donors was carried over to the new and fundamentally different technological environment with little or no discussion or evaluation.

In 1984, the policy was codified into law through passage of the National Organ Transplant Act, which expressly proscribes payment to organ donors or their surviving family members. As a result, the altruistic system was firmly locked into place without any serious inquiry regarding its effectiveness in the new environment of deceased organ donors. . . .

Ineffective Responses to the Organ Shortage

Aware of the increasingly dire consequences of continued reliance on the existing approach to cadaveric organ procurement and alarmed at the figures shown above, the transplant industry has examined and adopted a series of policy options ostensibly designed to improve the system's performance. All of these, however, continue to maintain the basic zero-price property of the altruistic system. As a result, the likelihood that any of them, even in combination, will resolve the organ shortage is remote.

Survey evidence indicates that less than 40 percent of U.S. citizens have signed their donor cards.

At least seven such actions have been implemented over the last two decades or so:

Increased Educational Expenditures

In the absence of financial incentives, moral suasion becomes the principal avenue through which additional supply may be motivated. Consequently, the organ procurement organizations (OPOs) created under the 1984 Act have launched substantial promotional campaigns. The campaigns have been designed to both educate the general public about the desperate need for donated organs and educate physicians and critical care hospital staff regarding the identification of potential deceased donors. Over the years, a substantial sum has been spent on these types of educational activities. Recent empirical evidence, however, suggests that further spending on these programs is unlikely to increase supply by a significant amount.

Organ Donor Cards

A related activity has been the process of incorporating organ donor cards on states' driver licenses. The cards can be easily completed and witnessed at the time the licenses are issued or renewed. They serve as a pre-mortem statement of the bearer's wish to have his or her organs removed for transplantation purposes at the time of death. Their principal use, in practice, is to facilitate the OPOs' efforts to convince surviving family members to consent to such removal by revealing the decedant's wishes.

The 1968 Uniform Anatomical Gift Act gave all states the authority to issue donor cards and incorporate them in drivers' licenses. Moreover, a few states have recently begun to rely entirely on donor cards to infer consent without requiring the surviving family's permission when such cards are present. Survey evidence indicates that less than 40 percent of U.S. citizens have signed their donor cards.

Required Request

Some survey evidence published in the late 1980s and early 1990s found that in a number of cases families of potential deceased donors were not being asked to donate the organs. As a result, donation was apparently failing to occur in some of those instances simply because the request was not being presented.

In response to this evidence, federal legislation was passed in 1987 requiring all hospitals receiving any federal funding (which, of course, is virtually all hospitals) to request organ donation in all deaths that occur under circumstances that would allow the deceased's organs to be used in transplantation. It appears that this legal obligation is now being met in most, if not all, cases. Yet, the organ shortage has persisted and the waiting list has continued to grow.

Required Referral

While required-request legislation can compel hospitals to approach the families of recently deceased potential organ donors with an appeal for donation, it cannot ensure that the request will be made in a sincere, compassionate manner likely to elicit an agreement. Following implementation of the required-request law, there were a number of anecdotes in which the compulsory organ donation requests were presented in an insincere or even offensive manner that was clearly intended to elicit a negative response. The letter of the law was being met but not the spirit. As a result, additional legislation was passed that requires hospitals to refer potential organ donors to the regional OPO so that trained procurement personnel can approach the surviving family with the donation request. This policy response has resulted in no perceptible progress in resolving the shortage.

Collaboration

A fairly recent response to the organ shortage has been the so-called "Organ Donation Breakthrough Collaborative," which was championed by then-secretary of health and human services Tommy Thompson. The program was initiated shortly after Thompson took office in 2001 and is currently continuing. The program's basic motivation is provided by the observation of a considerable degree of variation in performance across the existing OPOs. Specifically, the number of deceased organ donors per thousand hospital deaths has been found to vary by a factor of almost five across the organizations. The presumption, then, is that the relatively successful OPOs employ superior procurement techniques and/or knowledge that, if shared with the relatively unsuccessful organizations, would significantly improve their performance. Thus, diffusion of "best practice" techniques is seen as a promising method through which cadaveric donation rates may be greatly improved.

A thorough and objective evaluation of the Thompson initiative has not, to our knowledge, been conducted. . . . The good news is that the program appears to have had a positive (and potentially significant) impact on the number of donations. In particular, it appears that, after 2002, the growth rate of the waiting list has slowed somewhat. Whether this effect will permanently lower the growth rate of the waiting list or simply cause a temporary intercept shift remains to be seen. The bad news, however, is unequivocal—the initiative is not going to resolve the organ shortage. Even if, contrary to reasonable expectations, all OPO relative inefficiencies were miraculously eliminated (i.e., if all organizations' performance were brought up to the most efficient unit), the increase in donor collection rates would still be insufficient to eliminate the shortage.

Kidney Exchanges

Another approach that has received some attention recently involves the exchange of kidneys between families who have willing but incompatible living donors. Suppose, for example, a person in one family needs a kidney transplant and a sibling has offered to donate the needed organ. Further suppose that the two siblings are not compatible—perhaps their blood types differ. If this family can locate a second, similarly situated family, then it may be possible that the donor in the first family will match the recipient in the second, and vice versa. A relatively small number of such exchanges have recently occurred and a UNOS-based computerized system of matching such interfamily donors has been proposed to facilitate a larger number of these living donor transactions. . . .

It is quite apparent that living donor kidney exchanges are not going to resolve the organ shortage. Opportunities for such barter-based exchanges are simply too limited.

Reimbursement of Donor Costs

Finally, in another effort to encourage an increase in the number of living (primarily kidney) donors, several states have passed legislation authorizing reimbursement of any direct (explicit) costs incurred by such donors (e.g., travel expenses, lost wages, and so on). Economically, this policy action raises the price paid to living kidney donors from a negative amount to zero. As such, it should be expected to increase the quantity of organs supplied from this source.

Our concern is that every time another one of these marginalist policies is devised, it delays the only real reform that is capable of fully resolving the organ shortage.

Because the explicit, out-of-pocket expenses associated with live kidney donation are unlikely to be large relative to the longer-term implicit costs of potential health risks, however, such reimbursement should not be expected to bring forth a flood of new donors. Moreover, recent empirical evidence suggests that an increase in the number of living donors may have a negative impact on the number of deceased donors because of some degree of supply-side substitutability. Again, this policy is not a solution to the organ shortage.

We must conclude that none of the above-listed policies should be expected to resolve the transplant organ shortage. We say this not because we oppose any of these policies; indeed, each appears sensible in its own right and some have unquestionably succeeded in raising the number of organ donors by some (perhaps nontrivial) amount. Rather, our concern is that every time another one of these marginalist policies is devised, it delays the only real reform that is capable of fully resolving the organ shortage.

A cynical observer might easily conclude that the above string of largely ineffectual actions represents an intentional strategy of what might be termed "illusory responsiveness."

That is, the policies were never really intended or expected to resolve or even substantially ameliorate the organ shortage. Rather, they have been undertaken strategically to create the illusion that serious efforts were being made to address the issue while postponing more effective reforms. . . .

The Only Effective Solution

To an economist, the solution to this problem is both obvious and simple: repeal the National Organ Transplant Act and its progeny and allow the price of cadaveric organs to rise to equilibrium, market-clearing levels. While we cannot be certain exactly what the equilibrium prices would be, at least two economic considerations suggest that they are likely to be relatively low. First, there appears to be a large pool of excess capacity at current collection rates. Estimates suggest that we are presently harvesting only about half of the potential number of cadaveric donors. And second, the opportunity cost of cadaveric organ donation is quite low for most potential donors. Therefore, the price elasticity of supply of organs is likely to be quite large and the market clearing price is correspondingly low.

The medical community is increasingly confronted with the appalling consequences of a continued reliance on a policy that was originally adopted in a completely different technological environment.

A related issue pertaining to the supply of cadaveric organs involves the overall adequacy of this source of transplantable organs. Specifically, is there a sufficient number of deaths each year in the United States that occur under circumstances that would allow organ donation so as to resolve the shortage fully? The answer appears to be yes. . . .

There does appear to be a sufficiently large supply of potential cadaveric donors to resolve the shortage fully—that is, to stop adding to the waiting lists. Unfortunately, however, it will take years of surpluses to drain the backlog of excess demands that have accumulated from over 30 years of shortages—i.e., to eliminate the waiting lists. But the sooner we start doing so, the more lives will be saved. To continue to postpone the only effective solution in the unrealistic hope of resolving the shortage at a zero price is to condemn thousands more patients to death as they wait for organs that never arrive. . . .

Financial Incentives Appear Inevitable

Proposals to adopt financial incentives to foster an increased rate of cadaveric organ donation have now been forestalled for at least three decades. Opponents of such incentives have employed two strategies to postpone their use: repeated appeals to a set of alleged ethical concerns that upon closer inspection make no sense, and introduction of a parade of failed policy alternatives ostensibly intended to improve the current system while maintaining the zero-price constraint. Both approaches are wearing thin as the waiting list continues to grow and the number of deaths keeps rising.

The medical community is increasingly confronted with the appalling consequences of a continued reliance on a policy that was originally adopted in a completely different technological environment. As a result, the tide now seems to be turning and the adoption of financial incentives appears inevitable. The future costs of continued inaction are simply too large.

3

The Gap Between Supply and Demand for Organs Must Be Closed

The Economist

The Economist *is a weekly news and international affairs publication.*

The extreme organ shortage around the world has led to organ-harvesting scandals, organ trafficking, and illegal transplant tourism. In addition, the shortage has fueled the sale of diseased or decrepit human organs to unsuspecting patients. The shortage is caused, in part, by negative publicity about organs going to undeserving patients and by families who refuse to comply with the wishes of their deceased family member. Spain's system of presumed consent and Iran's policy of paying family members for organs have helped to close the gap in those countries.

As demand for life-saving transplant surgery grows, the idea of paying donors is gaining support.

"PLEASE don't take your organs to heaven," reads the American bumper sticker. "Heaven knows that we need them here on earth." Last year more than 7,000 Americans died while awaiting an organ transplant—almost double the number of American soldiers killed in Iraq since 2003. In Europe, too, thousands of people whose lives could be extended or transformed (by having sight restored, for example) through transplants forfeit the opportunity for want of available organs.

Research by the World Health Organisation (WHO) has found that only one in ten people in need of a new kidney, the body part most in demand, manages to get one. In the poorest places, of course, a complex transplant—which in the American health system costs $500,000—is unthinkable for most people anyway. But the gap between supply and demand for organs affects the poor too, by creating a market in body parts where abuses are rife.

Organ Shortages Lead to Organ Trafficking

In prosperous and middle-income countries, the waiting lists for organ transplants grow ever longer as ageing populations, hypertension and obesity (a big cause of diabetes-driven kidney failure) take their toll. The problem has been exacerbated by a fall in road deaths in rich countries, which—along with strokes and heart attacks—are the main source of organs for transplant. Small wonder that people scour the globe to procure the organs they or their loved ones need; or that unscrupulous intermediaries offer help.

> *Until very recently, a key destination for such "transplant tourists" was China, where ... there used to be a ready supply of organs plucked from the bodies of the thousands of people who are executed every year.*

The latest of many organ-harvesting scandals is now [2008] raging in India, one of several poor countries where the sale of organs used to be legal but has now been banned, with the apparent effect of driving the trade underground. A doctor, Amit Kumar, is awaiting trial after reportedly confessing to having performed hundreds of illegal transplants for rich clients from America, Britain, Canada, Saudi Arabia and Greece. He has been accused of luring labourers into his clinics with job offers; victims were then offered up to $2,000, a princely sum, to part with a kidney. Some who refused are said to have had kidneys removed anyway after being drugged.

Another kidney racket flourished in South Africa between 2001 and 2003. Donors were recruited in Brazil, Israel and Romania with offers of $5,000–20,000 to visit Durban and forfeit a kidney. The 109 recipients, mainly Israelis, each paid up to $120,000 for a "transplant holiday"; they pretended they were relatives of the donors and that no cash changed hands.

At least until very recently, a key destination for such "transplant tourists" was China, where—according to human-rights groups—there used to be a ready supply of organs plucked from the bodies of the thousands of people who are executed every year. China insisted that the prisoners' organs were only used with their "consent". But under global pressure, it agreed a year ago to stop the practice; in theory, only blood relatives of the executed can now get their organs. The sale of any human body part was banned in 2006. Before the change, about five Australians a year bought organs from the bodies of Chinese who had been executed, according to Jeremy Chapman, the Australian head of the International Transplantation Society. . . .

The risk of decrepit or diseased body parts being given to unsuspecting patients was highlighted by the revelation . . . that two American patients had died . . . after getting organs in 2007 from a teenager . . . [who] had a rare form of cancer.

Negative Publicity Discredits Transplants

Just why is there such a lack of donors in rich countries, given that, according to opinion polls, most people like the idea of donation and are ready in principle to participate? One big factor has been a stream of media reports that give people the impression of widespread malpractice by the medical profession and the funeral and biomedical industries.

These reports of shady activities do not always involve life-saving organs such as kidneys, hearts and livers. Michael Mastromarino, the leader of a New York body-snatching ring, was recently jailed for at least 18 years after stealing bones, skin, arterial valves, ligaments and other tissues from corpses nabbed from funeral homes. Most of these parts were used for dental implants, or hip or knee replacements. To avoid detection, the bodies would be "boned" below the waist; PVC piping was then sewed back on in time for open-casket wakes. The parts were afterwards sold on, without proper screening for disease, and used in more than 20,000 transplants. Mr Mastromarino, an ex-dental surgeon, made millions of dollars from the scam. Among his victims was Alistair Cooke, a British broadcaster who died in New York in 2004 at the age of 95.

Court hearings arising from the Mastromarino case, replete with gore, will run and run. Next month four employees of his biomedical firm, and the directors of three funeral homes that colluded with him, go on trial. In September [2008] a Philadelphia court was packed with relatives who were aghast as two brothers who ran funeral homes admitted selling their loved ones' parts to the Mastromarino ring. Separately, recipients of body parts from the racket have begun lawsuits on grounds that their lives have been endangered by "diseased" organs.

The risk of decrepit or diseased body parts being given to unsuspecting patients was highlighted by the revelation earlier this year that two American patients had died, and another two were undergoing chemotherapy, after getting organs in 2007 from a teenager who was thought to have died from meningitis but was later found to have had a rare form of cancer. The two recipients of his pancreas and his liver died from the same cancer. The publicity such cases attract—rare as they may be—risks discrediting the very idea of transplants. . . .

In America, nearly 30,000 organ transplants are now carried out per year: an average of 82 a day. The number of available organs is not keeping up. A record 100,000 Americans are on waiting lists, with 4,400 names being added each month. True, some sign up with two or more transplant units. But more than a quarter have been on waiting lists for at least three years; one in seven for five years or more. And the toll of avoidable deaths goes up and up.

Organ Distribution Can Go Away

Among American campaigners for organ donation, there were groans of dismay after an investigation by the Los Angeles Times found that four notorious Japanese criminals got transplants at the Medical Centre of the University of California Los Angeles, apparently jumping a queue of needy Americans. Without commenting on the report's details, the centre defended itself, saying it abided by the rules of the United Network for Organ Sharing (UNOS), a federally-mandated arrangement. This allows for some non-American recipients (up to 5%), since there are some non-American donors. The centre also pointed out that it has no mandate to make moral judgments about the people who get organs. But for Americans who might hope to bequeath their parts to a deserving compatriot, it is horrible to imagine a foreign gangster benefiting.

Most of the time, at least, America's 254 transplant centres stick to UNOS's strict rules on the use of organs. As in most countries, priority generally goes to children. Then several other factors come into play: compatibility between donor and recipient; geography (some organs last only a few hours after extraction); the urgency of need; the likely improvement in quality and length of a recipient's life. (A new kidney can extend the life of a robust patient by as much as 20 years.)

On this set of criteria, the over-70s are relegated to the back of the queue. But they are now the fastest-growing group on American waiting lists. In desperation, some turn to children or grandchildren for the kidney or liver part they need, according to Nancy Scheper-Hughes, an American medical anthropologist and campaigner against abuses in the organ trade. Normal selection criteria do not apply to voluntary donations between relatives. For sufferers from kidney failure, dialysis is possible—but at a cost of huge personal disruption and a gigantic bill.

When their loved ones die, 40% of Britons refuse to let their organs be removed, even if that is the express wish of the deceased.

In Britain more than 7,600 people are now waiting for various organs—nearly 50% up on just a decade ago. Despite a record 3,235 transplants in the 12 months up to March, nearly 500 patients died before a suitable donor was found. Three in four Britons tell pollsters they are ready to donate their organs when they die, yet only around a quarter are registered donors—and far fewer end up actually donating their parts. With barely 13 deceased donors per 1 [million], Britain's rate of "cadaveric" donation (ie, after death) is less than half Spain's or America's, and well below that of many other rich countries.

Family Objections Contribute to Organ Shortages

This partly reflects the high objection rate among British donors' relatives. When their loved ones die, 40% of Britons refuse to let their organs be removed, even if that is the express wish of the deceased. In Portugal, the refusal rate is only 6%.

In Britain, just as in America, news reports have sapped confidence in the transplant business. In recent weeks, eyebrows were raised after it emerged that part of a liver obtained through the National Health Service [NHS] was used for a private patient, a Kuwaiti boy, at King's College Hospital in London. The surgeon involved was cleared of any wrong-doing after explaining that he had given most of the liver to an NHS patient, while reserving the left lobe for the boy, who was critically ill.

A general British wariness about the abuse of body parts dates from a scandal at the Alder Hey children's hospital in Liverpool where Dick van Velzen, a Dutch pathologist, cut thousands of parts from children who died between 1988 and 1994, without their parents' knowledge. Although the parts were taken for research, not transplants, the outrage was huge.

A government-mandated inquiry into British transplants noted that despite a rise in living donors (mainly of kidneys) there has been a fall since 2002 in one critical indicator: the number of donations from bodies that are pronounced brain-dead but whose other organs (including heart and lungs) are still functioning.

A big reason for this is the objections raised by many families who could not bear the idea of loved ones' parts being removed from bodies that seemed to be working. The precise definition of death also concerns people who are less intimately involved. Although the world's main religions (including Islam and Roman Catholicism) endorse the idea of organ donation in order to save lives, some Christian theologians say doctors are too quick to call people "irreversibly brain-dead" when bits of the brain might still be operating.

Such sensitivities help explain why so many countries (including Britain) continue to have an "opt-in" system of donation, under which those willing to give their organs on death must sign up as donors, as opposed to the "presumed consent" or "opt-out" systems, under which everyone is assumed to be a donor unless they register an objection. In most opt-out systems, the next of kin's approval is also required. Spain, France, Italy and Austria, which have presumed consent, all have high deceased-donor rates, of over 20 per 1m; that's why Britain, too, is debating such a system. But presumed consent is no panacea. Greece, with an opt-out system, has low cadaveric-donor rates; America, with an opt-in system, ranks pretty high.

Iran began paying unrelated living donors for their kidneys in 1988. Just 11 years later it had eliminated its kidney-transplant waiting list—a feat no other country has achieved.

The Spanish System Increases Organ Donations

Spain, champion of the dead-donor league and pioneer of the opt-out approach, has more than doubled its rate (from 14 to 34) in the past 20 years. But that is not merely the result of an opt-out system; at least as much of Spain's success reflects an excellent network of organ-transplant teams in every hospital, which routinely screen patients' records to find potential donors. The recent British inquiry found that mainly by copying Spain's efficiency, donation could be boosted by 50%, enough to cover Britain's needs. Another factor is that Spain's media have helped allay public fears. Even so, Spain still has waiting lists; so it, like others, is increasingly looking to living donors as an alternative source of kidneys, liver parts and pancreas parts, which can be removed without any long-term harm to the donor's health. (The removal of a kidney is now pretty safe, that of liver parts less so.) Such transplants mostly take place between relatives or loved ones. Altruistic strangers also offer parts, but this is rare. . . .

Iran Closes the Gap Through Monetary Compensation

But it is Iran (with a low deceased-donor rate) that has the highest living-donor rate in the world—23 per 1m. It is also the only country where monetary compensation for organs is officially sanctioned. Iran began paying unrelated living donors for their kidneys in 1988. Just 11 years later it had eliminated its kidney-transplant waiting lists—a feat no other country has achieved. Under the Iranian system, a patient wanting a kidney must first seek a suitable, willing donor in his family. If that fails, he must wait up to six months for a suitable deceased donor.

Failing that, he can apply to the national transplant association for a kidney from a list of living donor volunteers. They are offered two forms of compensation: a fixed $1,200 fee plus free health insurance for one year from the government; and a lump sum from the recipient or, if he is too poor, from a designated charity, of between $2,300 and $4,500. In theory at least, foreigners can't be buyers or sellers.

In practice, Iran also has a market in kidneys (allowing buyers and sellers to agree a price that tops up the sums officially available). In addition, there are altruistic donors, who offer up kidneys anonymously as an Islamic duty, or in gratitude for a prayer that has been answered. In fact, Iran's reality runs the gamut of approaches from commerce to state support to kindness. It somehow works; Iranians no longer go abroad for kidneys.

In every other country, the trade in human organs is illegal, at least on paper. Even Pakistan, which along with China used to take the bulk of transplant tourists, decided last year to ban organ sales. Filipinos tried to fill the gap, openly advertising kidney "surgery" on the internet for $65,000–95,000—a fraction of the cost in America. In 2007 foreigners accounted for nearly half the kidney transplants in the Philippines. For a while, the government turned a blind eye. But in April it banned transplants for non-Filipinos.

The WHO has included the idea of a worldwide ban on the trade in organs in its latest draft of "Guiding Principles" for transplants, which have not been updated since 1991. Approved in May by the agency's executive board, the draft will go to its full assembly for final approval in June next year. Its position is stern and clear: the legal sale of organs is likely to exploit the poorest and weakest groups in society, to undermine altruistic giving and may also lead to human trafficking. But the rapidly worsening shortage of organs, particularly kidneys, has led some patients' groups, doctors and politicians to look again at some form of reward for living donors.

Some Doctors Favor Compensation

For example, Israel has passed a law to allow donors to be paid fixed compensation of around $5,100 for loss of earnings during transplant surgery and recuperation. (The Orthodox Jewish stress on the integrity of the human body has been one factor in the lowish rate of donations in Israel.) Benjamin Hippen, a transplant neurologist with the Carolinas Medical Centre in Charlotte, North Carolina, suggests that American donors be offered some reward, such as lifelong health insurance. The Netherlands has considered that too.

In 2005, Dr Hippen notes, 341,000 Americans were on dialysis, triple the number in 1988. This cost the state $21 billion a year, more than 6% of Medicare's total budget. By 2010, their number is expected to swell to around half a million, rising to perhaps 700,000 by 2020. Though Iran's system is "far from perfect", America could learn "a good deal" from it, he says.

Gavin Carney, a professor at Australia's National University Medical Hospital, suggests paying each donor around $47,000. This, he says, would save thousands of Australian lives and billions of dollars in the cost of care for patients, some of whom wait seven years for a kidney. The government "shouldn't just let people rot on dialysis", he says. Nadey Hakim, a London transplant surgeon and ex-president of the International College of Surgeons, also favours some form of compensation. "There really is no other option," he says.

4

Around the World, Innovative Programs Boost Organ Donations

Alex Tabarrok

Alex Tabarrok is a professor at George Mason University and a director of research for the Independent Institute.

Countries around the world are developing innovative ways of dealing with organ shortages. In Singapore and Iran, donors and their families receive financial compensation for organs. Israel has developed a system wherein those who do not register to be organ donors are placed at the bottom of the list should they someday need an organ themselves. In the US, doctors routinely harvest tissue such as corneas without family consent. Finally, many countries have established a policy of presumed consent; that is, a person is automatically considered an organ donor unless he or she has specified otherwise.

Harvesting human organs for sale! The idea suggests the lurid world of horror movies and 19th-century grave-robbers. Yet right now, Singapore is preparing to pay donors as much as 50,000 Singapore dollars (almost US$36,000) for their organs. Iran has eliminated waiting lists for kidneys entirely by paying its citizens to donate. Israel is implementing a "no give, no take" system that puts people who opt out of the donor system at the bottom of the transplant waiting list should they ever need an organ.

Alex Tabarrok, "The Meat Market," *The Wall Street Journal*, January 8, 2010, http://online.wsj.com. Copyright © 2010 by Alex Tabarrok. All rights reserved. Reproduced by permission.

Millions of people suffer from kidney disease, but in 2007 there were just 64,606 kidney-transplant operations in the entire world. In the U.S. alone, 83,000 people wait on the official kidney-transplant list. But just 16,500 people received a kidney transplant in 2008, while almost 5,000 died waiting for one.

Routine removal is perhaps the most extreme response to the devastating shortage of organs world-wide.

Routine Removal Is Legal

To combat yet another shortfall, some American doctors are routinely removing pieces of tissue from deceased patients for transplant without their, or their families', prior consent. And the practice is perfectly legal. In a number of U.S. states, medical examiners conducting autopsies may and do harvest corneas with little or no family notification. (By the time of autopsy, it is too late to harvest organs such as kidneys.) Few people know about routine removal statutes and perhaps because of this, these laws have effectively increased cornea transplants.

Routine removal is perhaps the most extreme response to the devastating shortage of organs world-wide. That shortage is leading some countries to try unusual new methods to increase donation. Innovation has occurred in the U.S. as well, but progress has been slow and not without cost or controversy.

The Disputed Line Between Life and Death

Organs can be taken from deceased donors only after they have been declared dead, but where is the line between life and death? Philosophers have been debating the dividing line between baldness and nonbaldness for over 2,000 years, so there is little hope that the dividing line between life and death will ever be agreed upon. Indeed, the great paradox of deceased donation is that we must draw the line between life and death precisely where we cannot be sure of the answer, because the line must lie where the donor is dead but the donor's organs are not.

In 1968 the Journal of the American Medical Association published its criteria for brain death. But reduced crime and better automobile safety have led to fewer potential brain-dead donors than in the past. Now, greater attention is being given to donation after cardiac death: no heart beat for two to five minutes (protocols differ) after the heart stops beating spontaneously. Both standards are controversial—the surgeon who performed the first heart transplant from a brain-dead donor in 1968 was threatened with prosecution, as have been some surgeons using donation after cardiac death. Despite the controversy, donation after cardiac death more than tripled between 2002 and 2006, when it accounted for about 8% of all deceased donors nationwide. In some regions, that figure is up to 20%.

New Ways of Increasing Organ Supply

The shortage of organs has increased the use of so-called expanded-criteria organs, or organs that used to be considered unsuitable for transplant. Kidneys donated from people over the age of 60 or from people who had various medical problems are more likely to fail than organs from younger, healthier donors, but they are now being used under the pressure. At the University of Maryland's School of Medicine five patients recently received transplants of kidneys that had either cancerous or benign tumors removed from them. Why would anyone risk cancer? Head surgeon Dr. Michael Phelan explained, "the ongoing shortage of organs from deceased donors, and the high risk of dying while waiting for a transplant, prompted five donors and recipients to push ahead with surgery." Expanded-criteria organs are a useful response to the shortage, but their use also means that the shortage is even worse than it appears because as the waiting list lengthens, the quality of transplants is falling.

Routine removal has been used for corneas but is unlikely to ever become standard for kidneys, livers or lungs. Nevertheless more countries are moving toward presumed consent. Under that standard, everyone is considered to be a potential organ donor unless they have affirmatively opted out, say, by signing a non-organ-donor card. Presumed consent is common in Europe and appears to raise donation rates modestly, especially when combined, as it is in Spain, with readily available transplant coordinators, trained organ-procurement specialists, round-the-clock laboratory facilities and other investments in transplant infrastructure.

The Iranian system and the black market demonstrate one important fact: The organ shortage can be solved by paying living donors. The Iranian system began in 1988 and eliminated the shortage of kidneys by 1999.

The British Medical Association has called for a presumed consent system in the U.K., and Wales plans to move to such a system this year. India is also beginning a presumed consent program that will start this year with corneas and later expand to other organs. Presumed consent has less support in the U.S. but experiments at the state level would make for a useful test.

Rabbis selling organs in New Jersey? Organ sales from poor Indian, Thai and Philippine donors? Transplant tourism? It's all part of the growing black market in transplants. Already, the black market may account for 5% to 10% of transplants world-wide. If organ sales are voluntary, it's hard to fault either the buyer or the seller. But as long as the market remains underground the donors may not receive adequate postoperative care, and that puts a black mark on all proposals to legalize financial compensation.

Iran Eliminates the Organ Shortage

Only one country, Iran, has eliminated the shortage of transplant organs—and only Iran has a working and legal payment system for organ donation. In this system, organs are not bought and sold at the bazaar. Patients who cannot be assigned a kidney from a deceased donor and who cannot find a related living donor may apply to the nonprofit, volunteer-run Dialysis and Transplant Patients Association (Datpa). Datpa identifies potential donors from a pool of applicants. Those donors are medically evaluated by transplant physicians, who have no connection to Datpa, in just the same way as are uncompensated donors. The government pays donors $1,200 and provides one year of limited health-insurance coverage. In addition, working through Datpa, kidney recipients pay donors between $2,300 and $4,500. Charitable organizations provide remuneration to donors for recipients who cannot afford to pay, thus demonstrating that Iran has something to teach the world about charity as well as about markets.

The Iranian system and the black market demonstrate one important fact: The organ shortage can be solved by paying living donors. The Iranian system began in 1988 and eliminated the shortage of kidneys by 1999. Writing in the Journal of Economic Perspectives in 2007, Nobel Laureate economist Gary Becker and Julio Elias estimated that a payment of $15,000 for living donors would alleviate the shortage of kidneys in the U.S. Payment could be made by the federal government to avoid any hint of inequality in kidney allocation. Moreover, this proposal would save the government money since even with a significant payment, transplant is cheaper than the dialysis that is now paid for by Medicare's End Stage Renal Disease program.

In March 2009 Singapore legalized a government plan for paying organ donors. Although it's not clear yet when this will be implemented, the amounts being discussed for payment, around $50,000, suggest the possibility of a significant donor incentive. So far, the U.S. has lagged other countries in addressing the shortage, but last year, Sen. Arlen Specter circulated a draft bill that would allow U.S. government entities to test compensation programs for organ donation. These programs would only offer noncash compensation such as funeral expenses for deceased donors and health and life insurance or tax credits for living donors.

World-wide we will soon harvest more kidneys from living donors than from deceased donors. In one sense, this is a great success—the body can function perfectly well with one kidney so with proper care, kidney donation is a low-risk procedure. In another sense, it's an ugly failure. Why must we harvest kidneys from the living, when kidneys that could save lives are routinely being buried and burned? A payment of funeral expenses for the gift of life or a discount on driver's license fees for those who sign their organ donor card could increase the supply of organs from deceased donors, saving lives and also alleviating some of the necessity for living donors.

Presumed consent, financial compensation for living and deceased donors and point systems would all increase the supply of transplant organs. Too many people have died already but pressure is mounting for innovation that will save lives.

The No Give, No Take Policy Works

Two countries, Singapore and Israel, have pioneered nonmonetary incentives systems for potential organ donors. In Singapore anyone may opt out of its presumed consent system. However, those who opt out are assigned a lower priority on the transplant waiting list should they one day need an organ, a system I have called "no give, no take."

Many people find the idea of paying for organs repugnant but they do accept the ethical foundation of no give, no take—that those who are willing to give should be the first to receive. In addition to satisfying ethical constraints, no give, no take increases the incentive to sign one's organ donor card thereby reducing the shortage. In the U.S., Lifesharers.org, a nonprofit network of potential organ donors (for which I am an adviser), is working to implement a similar system.

In Israel a more flexible version of no give, no take will be phased into place beginning this year. In the Israeli system, people who sign their organ donor cards are given points pushing them up the transplant list should they one day need a transplant. Points will also be given to transplant candidates whose first-degree relatives have signed their organ donor cards or whose first-degree relatives were organ donors. In the case of kidneys, for example, two points (on a 0- to 18-point scale) will be given if the candidate had three or more years previous to being listed signed their organ card. One point will be given if a first-degree relative has signed and 3.5 points if a first-degree relative has previously donated an organ.

The world-wide shortage of organs is going to get worse before it gets better, but we do have options. Presumed consent, financial compensation for living and deceased donors and point systems would all increase the supply of transplant organs. Too many people have died already but pressure is mounting for innovation that will save lives.

5

Registered Donors Should Have Priority Access to Organs for Transplant

Katrina A. Bramstedt

Katrina A. Bramstedt is a formally trained transplant ethicist.

In the face of severe organ shortages, organ allocation presents a difficult ethical conundrum. People who are willing to receive an organ if needed, but who do not register to be donors themselves are called "free riders." Thus, one proposal concerning organ allocation is to prioritize those who are registered organ donors above non-donors on the transplant waiting lists. Lifesharers, an organization in the United States, is a voluntary network of registered donors who specify that their organs should go to other members of Lifesharers in need of transplants upon their deaths. This system favors those who are willing to give.

Each year, thousands of patients who are on the United Network for Organ Sharing (UNOS) transplant waiting lists die, as the number of allografts that become available do not meet the demand. Some patients wait months or years for an organ, depending on blood type, body size, geographic location, and organ needed. As of December 1, 2005, there were more than 90000 people waiting for an organ transplant in the United States, and some of these patients need more than 1 type of organ. Yearly, there are approximately 6300 deceased

Katrina A. Bramstedt, "Is it Ethical to Prioritize Patients for Organ Allocation According to Their Values about Organ Donation?" *Progress in Transplantation*, vol. 16., no. 2, June 2006, pp. 170–173. Copyright © 2006 by North American Transplant Coordinators Organization (NATCO). All rights reserved. Reproduced by permission.

donors who provide an average of 3 organs for transplantation. UNOS estimates that roughly 50% of eligible deaths result in organ donation. Further, donation rates have increased only 3% each year from 1994 to 2003, despite efforts to educate society about the need for organ donation, and the use of donor registry campaigns, at United States motor vehicle registration offices.

As patients wait for donor organs, they risk further clinical deterioration that can render them unsuitable for transplantation. To address these lengthy waiting periods, some patients seek living donors or bridging devices. Some patients use the media or the Internet to announce their organ need. Another option is multiple listing; that is, placement on waiting lists at numerous hospitals to increase the chance to receive a transplant. This latter option is usually available only to those who have the financial means for multiple transplant candidacy evaluations and live within a short distance from multiple transplant centers, or have the ability to hire charter aircraft for transport on short notice when an organ becomes available.

Prioritizing Organ Allocation

Several models of priority organ allocation (preferred status) have been proposed in the recent past, the first in the form of a letter to the editor in the *Wall Street Journal*. In this letter, attorney Jonathan Kaufelt proposed that a way of increasing organ donation would be to give transplant preference to those who have registered to be organ donors. This model has also been proposed by others. An extreme form of this concept has been proposed by Rupert Jarvis, a former researcher at the University of Swansea (United Kingdom). He argues that in a setting of scarce organs, only those who have registered their desire to be an organ donor should be allowed to be organ recipients. In all of these proposals, the central theme is that those who do not agree to participate in organ donation are free-riders—people willing to receive organs without being willing to give them. All proposals also project that the concept of preferred status will result in more people registering to be organ donors so as to have a competitive edge over others if they ever need a transplant.

In reality, preferred status for those willing to be organ donors already occurs in the United States and elsewhere. In Singapore, the government enforces a 1987 law that mandates priority organ allocation to those who opt-in as organ donors. Eurotransplant kidney allocation procedures reflect on the ratio of donations and transplantations occurring in each member country (Austria, Belgium, Germany, Luxembourg, The Netherlands, and Slovenia) to create a balance sheet. A negative balance means that the country is procuring more organs from its residents than it is transplanting. The patients in each country receive point allotments that reflect on the country's own kidney donation rate. Of note, it has been posed that in addition to the points based on the country's donation rate, bonus points be allotted to patients who had expressed personal willingness to be organ donors, but this has not been adopted.

In 1993, UNOS expressed concern that preferred status for those willing to be organ donors could create the perception that organ donation status is related to a person's moral worth, even though in reality, signing up for organ donation is a social contract. Further, they fear that preferred status for those registered as organ donors might be the beginning of a trend for other types of moral worth variables to enter the organ allocation equation. Others have had similar fears that focus on preferred status reduces the "pure charity" of organ donation to a form of exchange—the net effect being a tarnishing of the altruism of organ donation. Even with their concerns, UNOS did pose that a trial of preferred status could be employed; however, there are no reports that such a trial was ever initiated.

Although UNOS does not give preferred status to those who have registered as potential deceased organ donors, UNOS does give organ allocation preference to people who have been living donors (kidney, liver segment, lung segment, partial pancreas, small bowel segment). Specifically, 4 extra points are given to such individuals if they become listed for kidney transplantation themselves. It would seem that UNOS could extend the same concept to other organ transplantations. Although the listing systems are different across organ types, it is likely that a similar conceptual approach could be created. Their choice to recognize only living donors for prioritization and not those who consent to be deceased donors may reflect the fact that these individuals have subjected themselves to personal risk (while alive) for the benefit of others. The bonus points allocated by UNOS are similar to the point allocation scheme argued for by [researchers G.]. Gubernatis and [H.] Kliemt; namely, those who have been living kidney donors would receive the most bonus points when they, themselves, are in need of kidney transplantation.

Currently, about 70% of patients receiving organs from deceased donors in the United Sates are not registered as organ donors themselves.

The LifeSharers Model

An innovation in preferred status is the directed donation plan designed by an organization called LifeSharers. Directed donation is allowed by federal and state law (and UNOS), although some restrictions may apply in certain states. Founded in 2002, LifeSharers is a nonprofit voluntary network of organ donors. Members promise to donate their organs upon their death, and they give fellow members first access to their organs. LifeSharers applies only to deceased donation. As the member pool grows, members themselves have an increasing chance at receiving a donated organ if they should ever need one. Individuals registered with the organization carry a wallet card that signifies their directed donation to LifeSharers members as first priority. Individuals can also attach an addendum to their advance directive/durable power of attorney documents indicating their membership and wishes about directed donation. A phone call to LifeSharers will inform transplant teams and donor families about current LifeSharers members who are in need of a donor organ (in order of their ranking on the UNOS waiting list). If there is no match, the organ(s) are then allocated to nonmembers. Children can be members if they are enrolled by a parent or guardian.

Currently, about 70% of patients receiving organs from deceased donors in the United States are not registered as organ donors themselves. The foundational philosophy of Life-Sharers is that giving organs first to those consenting to be organ donors creates the incentive for people to become organ donors. Potential recipients must hold LifeSharers membership for 180 days before they qualify for first access to organs of other members. This waiting period discourages people from waiting to join only when they learn they need a transplant. As of November 30, 2005, LifeSharers reports nearly 3500 members, with 22 of these members listed on the UNOS transplant waiting list. These listed members will get first chance at any organs donated by deceased LifeSharers members. With the current membership volume, there is roughly a 16% chance that one or more LifeSharers members will die in the next 12 months in circumstances permitting recovery of an organ. LifeSharers projects 40000 members by summer 2006 because of their plan for increased marketing of their program.[1] At that volume, the potential for donation increases from 16% to 90%. This would facilitate the first member-to-member transplantation by possibly 2007.

LifeSharers presents a level playing field for all members as the "benefit" offered is the same for everyone, no matter their

1. In June 2011, LifeSharers reported a membership of 14,700.

age, gender, ethnicity, religion, or financial status. In fact, the only benefit is the potential, for priority organ allocation amid the concept of directed donation. There is no membership fee to join the organization, and no option to pay for additional benefits. In addition, the LifeSharers philosophy can potentially motivate people to become organ donors, something that benefits even nonmembers who are waiting for a transplant, because they too are potentially exposed to more organ matches. A net increase in organs available for transplantation will exist, because not all organs donated by LifeSharers members will match with LifeSharers patients who are waiting for transplants. . . .

Because organ transplantation is not a human right, and organs are very scarce, viewing free riders as having a lower priority in organ allocation is ethically permissible.

Free Riders and Society

The concept of free riders is ethically troublesome. An analogy is the UNOS restriction on the yearly amount of transplantations allowed to nonresident aliens. Many of these recipients are people who come to the United States for the sole purpose of receiving an organ transplant—unlikely to ever have been registered as organ donors in the United States (givers), rather only participating as recipients (takers) who return to their country of origin after transplantation. Similarly, organs from deceased donors in the United States can be exported to another country only if no suitable match is found in the United States. These policies support the notion of a "transplant community" with a foundation that reflects on the concepts of solidarity and reciprocity. These concepts are also foundational to models of preferred status that are based on organ donor registration.

In a setting in which preferred status is operational amid an allocation program that does not consider medical urgency, those who actively choose not to register as organ donors place themselves in a position of lower priority for organ allocation. Because organ transplantation is not a human right, and organs are very scarce, viewing free riders as having a lower priority in organ allocation is ethically permissible. Although the majority of polled members of the International Society for Heart and Lung Transplantation disagree, those with bona fide religious and/or moral objections to donation should not be subjected to the rules of a preferred status system, because they should be viewed as having a "special value" that is appropriate to respect.

People who cannot themselves consent to organ donation (children, adults lacking decision-making capacity) should also not be subjected to the rules of a preferred status system. Families may refuse to allow their children to be deceased organ donors, yet the child might hold values for organ donation that cannot legally be expressed because of minor age. The same can be said for guardians who refuse to allow adults under their charge to be deceased organ donors. These incompetent adults also cannot give legal consent to donate; thus, donation status should not be a variable to their transplant listing status. There should be no room for third parties to make decisions on behalf of patients who cannot decide for themselves, if those decisions could lower patients' waiting status.

In 2003, Dr Aaron Spital conducted a national telephone survey with regard to public attitudes about the concept of preferred status in organ allocation. Specifically, 1014 adults were asked, "Should people who have agreed to donate their organs after death be given priority to receive organs if they themselves should ever need them over people who have not agreed to donate their organs after death?" The majority of respondents reported "yes" or "probably yes" (53% of the total responses). Forty-one percent responded that priority should not or probably should not be given to those who would donate. Interestingly, those who were college educated were less supportive of this plan than those who were less educated. Younger people were generally more supportive of the plan than older people. Thirteen years earlier, UNOS conducted a similar telephone survey involving 800 adults. Their survey was worded such that bonus points allotted for willingness to be an organ donor would not override situations of medical urgency. Of the 52% of respondents who supported financial or nonfinancial incentives to increase the rate of organ donation, most indicated they favored preferred status as the form of incentive. The results of these studies indicate that society would, at a minimum, likely support a UNOS sponsored trial of a preferred status program. The program timeline should be of sufficient length so as to allow for monitoring of donation trends.

Organ Donors Should Have Preferred Access to Organs

Increasing the number of organ donors without the aspect of changing the order of those waiting in the queue would be the optimal approach for transplant medicine; however, historically this has not occurred and donor projections (3% yearly increase) do not predict that such will materialize. Faced with dismal organ donation rates and projections, the LifeSharers approach is ethically permissible, yet it could be enhanced by a waiting period exception clause as discussed above. Although some may term LifeSharers a "club," it is nonetheless a club that is open to children as well as adults with decision-making capacity, with no membership fee. It also avoids the ethically problematic matters of active solicitation of donors using the media, as well as financial incentives for organ donation.

Does LifeSharers play favorites? Yes. And in the case of organ scarcity it is appropriate to favor fellow organ donors (actual or prospective) over free riders. When it is time to allocate a scare resource, it is fair to assign priority to people who are willing to both give and receive. Preferred status does not need to operate merely as a tiebreaker when all other variables are equal. Further, preferred status should not cease to operate when nonpreferred patients are more severely ill, because this would devalue willingness to donate.

6

Younger Patients Should Have Priority Access to Organs for Transplantation

Katie Moisse

Katie Moisse is a reporter for the ABC News Medical Unit.

Under the current system, age and health status does not affect a person's standing on the organ transplant waiting lists, according to United Network for Organ Sharing (UNOS) guidelines. Many feel that the guidelines are unfair and should be changed so that older or ill recipients do not receive organs that would outlast their expected life spans. Rather, younger patients, who have the longest expected life spans, should receive the healthiest and youngest organs while older patients, who have shorter expected life spans, should receive older or less healthy organs.

Jerry Powell's kidneys may be dying, but the 50-year-old newlywed still has a lot of living to do. Within weeks, Powell will rely on dialysis to filter his blood. And ultimately, he'll need a kidney transplant. But the United Network for Organ Sharing (UNOS)—the organization charged with allocating the nation's organs—is considering a policy change that could impact Powell's standing.

Currently, those at the top of an 87,000-strong waiting list are next in line for a matched kidney—regardless of age and health status.

The Current System Is Unfair

"We started with what we thought was best at the time, but as things change we need to make improvements," said Dr. Christopher Marsh, chief of transplant surgery at the Scripps Center for Organ and Cell Transplantation and UNOS board member. "The current system is not fair. The new approach, from a medical and scientific standpoint, is an improvement."

When faced with the prospect of rationing, the ethical responsibility is to use resources prudently and save the most lives and years of life.

The proposed change, which was released as a concept document Feb. 16 for public comment, would reserve 20 percent of donor organs for those receipients expected to live the longest after a transplant, and the remaining 80 percent for recipients age-matched to within 15 years of the donor.

"This would reduce the possibility that a candidate reasonably expected to live ten more years receives a kidney that may function for 40 years, or conversely that a candidate reasonably expected to live 40 more years receives a kidney that may function for only ten," Anne Paschke a spokeswoman for UNOS, said in a statement.

Only 17,000 Americans receive a transplant each year, and more than 4,600 die waiting.

"When faced with the prospect of rationing, the ethical responsibility is to use resources prudently and save the most lives and years of life," said Arthur Caplan, chair of medical ethics at the University of Pennsylvania. "It's the policy we follow during war: help those most likely to recover without doctors and intensive care beds. The sicker you are, the less likely you are to do well with a transplant."

A Need for Change

Although the proposal was only recently made public, the idea has been around for almost a decade.

"It's been a long process," Marsh said. "We've come up with ideas and run up against barriers. Change is difficult, and patients and programs are used to a simple allocation system."

"Every policy change is always disconcerting because there are new winners and new losers," said Dr. Antonio Di Carlo, assistant professor at the University of Vermont College of Medicine and chief of transplant surgery at Fletcher Allen Healthcare.

According to the 40-page proposal, people over 50 would lose an advantage they currently hold. The donor pool for a 60-year-old could theoretically be cut by half.

"No matter how you look at it, there will be some people advantaged fairly and disadvantaged unfairly. But the same thing goes with the current policy. It's not right to have someone die with a pristine kidney while a young person needs two or three transplants throughout their lifetime."

For patients like Powell, the change could mean getting an older kidney with fewer functional years. It could also mean getting an "extended criteria donation"—a kidney that, until recent years, would not have been transplanted at all.

"I think it my particular case, it would limit my options," Powell said.

7

Teens Undergoing Organ Transplants Do Not Fare As Well As Older Patients

Lauran Neergaard

Lauran Neergaard covers health and medical issues for the Associated Press in Washington, DC.

Teenagers sometimes have a difficult time with the knowledge they need an organ transplant; often they are in denial or are angry about their situation. Although teens do very well during the first year after surgery, often adolescents do less well in the long-term. Either through rebelliousness or difficulty with the side effects of medication, teens sometimes fail to carry through on the complicated care regimen required after an organ transplant. Sometimes meeting another teen who has gone through a similar surgery can provide much needed support.

Courtney Montgomery's heart was failing fast, but the 16-year-old furiously refused when her doctors, and her mother, urged a transplant.

Previous surgeries hadn't helped and the North Carolina girl didn't believe this scarier operation would either. It would take another teen who's thriving with a new heart to change her mind.

"I was like, 'No, I don't want this. If I'm going to die, I'm going to die,'" Courtney recalls. "Now I look back, I realize I wasn't thinking the way I should have been."

Caring for Teen Transplant Patients Is Complex

Teenagers can add complex psychology to organ transplantation: Even though they're minors, they need to be on board with a transplant because it's up to them to take care of their new organ. Depression, anger and normal adolescent pangs—that tug-of-war with parents, trying to fit in—can interfere. It's not just a question of having the transplant, but how motivated they are to stick with anti-rejection treatment for years to come.

"The decision-making process that we go through, in terms of our ability to weigh factors in a rational sense, probably doesn't mature until you're in your late 20s," says Dr. Robert Jaquiss, pediatric heart surgery chief at Duke University Medical Center, where Courtney eventually was transplanted. "It introduces an enormous level of complexity to caring for these kids."

One study found up to 40 percent of adolescent liver recipients eventually miss medication doses or checkups.

Then there's the sense of isolation. Far fewer adolescents than older adults undergo an organ transplant, making it unlikely that a teen has ever seen how fast their peers can bounce back.

Between 700 and 800 adolescents, ages 11 to 17, have some type of organ transplant each year. That's nearly 40 percent of the roughly 2,000 annual pediatric transplants. Teens fare better than any other age—child or adult—the first year after surgery. But long-term, adolescents do a bit worse than younger children, and the reason isn't biological, Jaquiss says. It's that teens, and young adults as well, tend to start slipping on all the required follow-up care.

Teens Miss Medications

One study found up to 40 percent of adolescent liver recipients eventually miss medication doses or checkups. It can be normal development, as teens start sleeping late and simply forgetting morning doses, or sometimes it's rebelliousness. Then there are medication side effects that Jaquiss says can be especially troubling to this image-conscious age group: weight gain, acne and unwanted hair growth.

And at the Children's Hospital of Pittsburgh, separate research with heart recipients has found chronological age is unrelated to "medical maturity." Young patients who had a hard time accepting a transplant as normal and who avoided family discussion of problems, for example, were less likely to stick with care.

Courtney's mother, Michelle Mescall, said that when the medical center advised that her daughter needed to agree to go on the transplant waiting list, "I said, 'Well she's a minor, what do you mean? I'm going to make this decision.' I was just floored that it was now her decision."

Legally, the hospital could have proceeded with mom's OK. But clinical social worker Shani Foy-Watson says if that happened, Courtney's resentment could have torpedoed her recovery, setting up just those kinds of problems with follow-up care.

Foy-Watson says it's not unusual for kids who've lived with serious illness for years to have a hard time imagining normalcy—at the same age when it's normal to seek more independence from their terrified parents.

Courtney, of Asheville, N.C., was diagnosed at age 8 with hypertrophic cardiomyopathy, a thickened and hard-to-pump heart that's the leading cause of sudden death in young athletes. Her mother tried to shield her from doctors' death warnings, but says Courtney became anxious and depressed early on.

She had a defibrillator implanted and later heart surgery that offered only temporary relief, fueling resentment of her mother's medical choices. Courtney eventually had to give up her beloved cheerleading, and last year required home-schooling.

Peer Support Helps Teens

As a few weeks passed with Courtney still resisting a transplant, the social worker tried a new tack: A 17-year-old football player had received a new heart at Duke a few months earlier because of the same condition, and already was back at school in Raleigh. Would he meet with Courtney?

It was a gamble. No one told Josh Winstead, now 18, the reason for the meeting, and they might not have hit it off. But they did, and Courtney immediately changed her mind.

"I guess me doing what I do, being a kid, helped out the most," says Winstead, who took Courtney to his prom a week before her surgery. "It was more just showing her how normal my life is."

You hear all the advice from friends and doctors, Courtney says, "but it doesn't hit home like when Josh would tell me, 'I have the same scars you do and this is how it felt and this is how I feel now.'"

She got her new heart last month. She's recovering well and exercising in hopes of getting back to the cheerleading squad.

Her mother's helping Courtney learn to handle a whopping 33 pills a day, and is proud of how her daughter has rallied: "I'm just dealing with how to let go and let her fly, but also be the parent of a 16-year-old."

8

Illegal Organ Trafficking Is a Serious Global Problem

Jeneen Interlandi

Jeneen Interlandi is a reporter for Newsweek *magazine.*

Anthropologist Nancy Scheper-Hughes has tracked the illegal sales of human organs around the world, including in the United States, where she believes surgeons are unwittingly using organs procured through the black market. The World Health Organization believes that organ selling is a serious problem. In one instance, an Israeli man who wanted to visit the US arranged to sell a kidney to finance the trip. In other cases, women were forced to sell kidneys to help support their families. Although some action has been taken, the illegal trade continues to flourish.

By the time her work brought her back to the United States, Nancy Scheper-Hughes had spent more than a decade tracking the illegal sale of human organs across the globe. Posing as a medical doctor in some places and a would-be kidney buyer in others, she had linked gangsters, clergymen and surgeons in a trail that led from South Africa, Brazil and other developing nations all the way back to some of her own country's best medical facilities. So it was that on an icy February afternoon in 2003, the anthropologist from the University of California, Berkeley, found herself sitting across from a group of transplant surgeons in a small conference room at a big Philadelphia hospital.

US Surgeons Engage in Black-Market Organ Transplants

By accident or by design, she believed, surgeons in their unit had been transplanting black-market kidneys from residents of the world's most impoverished slums into the failing bodies of wealthy dialysis patients from Israel, Europe and the United States. According to Scheper-Hughes, the arrangements were being negotiated by an elaborate network of criminals who kept most of the money themselves. For about $150,000 per transplant, these organ brokers would reach across continents to connect buyers and sellers, whom they then guided to "broker-friendly" hospitals here in the United States (places where Scheper-Hughes says surgeons were either complicit in the scheme or willing to turn a blind eye). The brokers themselves often posed as or hired clergy to accompany their clients into the hospital and ensure that the process went smoothly. The organ sellers typically got a few thousand dollars for their troubles, plus the chance to see an American city.

> *International organ trafficking. . . is flourishing; the World Health Organization estimates that one fifth of the 70,000 kidneys transplanted worldwide every year come from the black market.*

As she made her case, Scheper-Hughes, a diminutive 60-something with splashes of pink in her short, grayish-brown hair, slid a bulky document across the table—nearly 60 pages of interviews she had conducted with buyers, sellers and brokers in virtually every corner of the world. "People all over were telling me that they didn't have to go to a Third World hospital, but could get the surgery done in New York, Philadelphia or Los Angeles," she says. "At top hospitals, with top surgeons." In interview after interview, former transplant patients had cited the Philadelphia hospital as a good place to go for brokered transplants. Two surgeons in the room had also been named repeatedly. Scheper-Hughes had no idea if those surgeons were aware that some of their patients had bought organs illegally. She had requested the meeting so that she could call the transgression to their attention, just in case.

Hospital officials told *Newsweek* that after meeting with Scheper-Hughes, they conducted an internal review of their transplant program. While they say they found no evidence of wrongdoing on the part of their surgeons, they did tighten some regulations, to ensure better oversight of foreign donors and recipients. "But that afternoon," Scheper-Hughes says, "they basically threw me out."

It's little wonder. The exchange of human organs for cash or any other "valuable consideration" (such as a car or a vacation) is illegal in every country except Iran. Nonetheless, international organ trafficking—mostly of kidneys, but also of half-livers, eyes, skin and blood—is flourishing; the World Health Organization estimates that one fifth of the 70,000 kidneys transplanted worldwide every year come from the black market. Most of that trade can be explained by the simple laws of supply and demand. Increasing life spans, better diagnosis of kidney failure and improved surgeries that can be safely performed on even the riskiest of patients have spurred unprecedented demand for human organs. In America, the number of people in need of a transplant has nearly tripled during the past decade, topping 100,000 for the first time last October. But despite numerous media campaigns urging more people to mark the backs of their driver's licenses, the number of traditional (deceased) organ donors has barely budged, hovering between 5,000 and 8,000 per year for the last 15 years.

A Brutal New Calculus

In that decade and a half, a new and brutal calculus has emerged: we now know that a kidney from a living donor will keep you alive twice as long as one taken from a cadaver. And thanks to powerful antirejection drugs, that donor no longer needs to be an immediate family member (welcome news to those who would rather not risk the health of a loved one). In fact, surgeons say that a growing number of organ transplants are occurring between complete strangers. And, they acknowledge, not all those exchanges are altruistic. "Organ selling has become a global problem," says Frank Delmonico, a surgery professor at Harvard Medical School and adviser to the WHO. "And it's likely to get much worse unless we confront the challenges of policing it."

For Scheper-Hughes, the biggest challenge has been convincing people that the problem exists at all. "It used to be a joke that came up at conferences and between surgeons," she says. "In books and movies, you find these stories of people waking up in bathtubs full of ice with a scar where one of their kidneys used to be. People assumed it was just science fiction." That assumption has proved difficult to dismantle. In the mid-1980s, rumors that Americans were kidnapping children throughout Central America only to harvest their organs led to brutal attacks on American tourists in the region. When those stories proved false, the State Department classified organ-trafficking reports under "urban legend." Scheper-Hughes's evidence, which is largely anecdotal and comes in part from interviews with known criminals, has not convinced department officials otherwise. "It would be impossible to successfully conceal a clandestine organ-trafficking ring," Todd Leventhal, the department's countermisinformation officer, wrote in a 2004 report, adding that stories like the ones Scheper-Hughes tells are "irresponsible and totally unsubstantiated." In recent years, however, the WHO, Human Rights Watch and many transplant surgeons have broken with that view and acknowledged organ trafficking as a real problem.

At first, not even Scheper-Hughes believed the rumors. It was in the mid-1980s, during a study of infant mortality in the shantytowns of northern Brazil, that she initially caught wind of mythical "body snatcher" stories: vans of English-speaking foreigners would circle a village rounding up street kids whose bodies would later be found in trash bins removed of their livers, eyes, kidneys and hearts.

In Brazil, Africa, and Moldova, newspapers advertised the sale and solicitation of human body parts while brokers trolled the streets with $100 bills, easily recruiting young sellers.

When colleagues in China, Africa and Colombia reported similar rumblings, Scheper-Hughes began poking around. Some stories—especially the ones about kidnapped children, stolen limbs and tourists murdered for organs—were clearly false. But it was also clear that slums throughout the developing world were full of AWOL soldiers, desperate parents and anxious teenage boys willing to part with a kidney or a slice of liver in exchange for cash and a chance to see the world—or at least to buy a car.

Transplant Tourism and Organ Trafficking

Before long, Scheper-Hughes had immersed herself in an underworld of surgeons, criminals and those eager to buy or sell whatever body parts could be spared. In Brazil, Africa and Moldova, newspapers advertised the sale and solicitation of human body parts while brokers trolled the streets with $100 bills, easily recruiting young sellers. In Istanbul, Scheper-Hughes posed as an organ buyer and talked one would-be seller down to $3,000 for his "best kidney." In some of these countries, as the WHO later quantified, 60 to 70 percent of all transplant surgeries involved the transfer of organs from those countries' citizens to "transplant tourists" who came from the developed world.

But not all organs flowed from poor countries to rich ones; Americans, for example, were both buyers and sellers in this global market. A Kentucky woman once contacted Scheper-Hughes looking to sell her kidney or part of her liver so that she could buy some desperately needed dentures. And a Brooklyn dialysis patient purchased his kidney from Nick Rosen, an Israeli man who wanted to visit America.

Unlike some organ sellers, who told of dingy basement hospitals with less equipment than a spartan kitchen, Rosen found an organ broker through a local paper in Tel Aviv who arranged to have the transplant done at Mount Sinai Medical Center in New York. An amateur filmmaker, Rosen documented a portion of his odyssey on camera and sent the film to Scheper-Hughes, whose research he had read about online. The video excerpt that *Newsweek* viewed shows Rosen meeting his broker and buyer in a New York coffee shop where they haggle over price, then entering Mount Sinai and talking with surgeons—one of whom asks him to put the camera away. Finally, after displaying his post-surgery scars for the camera, Rosen is seen rolling across a hotel bed covered in $20 bills; he says he was paid $15,000. (Brokers, on the other hand, typically net around $50,000 per transplant, after travel and other expenses. In America, some insurance plans will cover at least a portion of the donor's medical expenses.)

In India, . . . women were being forced by their husbands to sell organs to foreign buyers in order to contribute to family income, or to provide for the dowry of a daughter.

The money changed hands outside the hospital's corridors, and Rosen says that he deliberately misled the Mount Sinai doctors, but that no one there challenged him. "One hospital in Maryland screened us out," he says. Tom Diflo, a transplant surgeon at New York University's Langone Medical Center, points out that many would-be donors do not pass the psychological screening, and that attempting to film the event would probably have set off an alarm bell or two. "But the doctors at Mount Sinai were not very curious about me," Rosen says. "We told them I was a close friend of the guy who I sold my kidney to, and that I was donating altruistically, and that was pretty much the end of it." Citing privacy laws, Mount Sinai officials declined to comment on the details of Rosen's case. But spokesperson Ian Michaels says that the hospital's screening process is rigorous and comprehensive, and assesses each donor's motivation. "All donors are clearly advised that it is against the law to receive money or gifts for being an organ donor," he says. "The pretransplant evaluation may not detect premeditated and skillful attempts to subvert and defraud the evaluation process."

Because many people do donate organs out of kindness, altruism provides an easy cover for those seeking to profit. And U.S. laws can be easy to circumvent, especially for foreign patients who may pay cash and are often gone in the space of a day. Diflo, who has worked in numerous transplant wards over the past two decades, says that while they are in the minority, hospitals that perform illegal transplants certainly exist in the United States. "There are a couple places around that have reputations for doing transplants with paid donors, and then some hospitals that have a 'don't ask, don't tell' policy," he says. "It's definitely happening, but it's difficult to ferret out."

Reliable Data Are Scarce

Diflo became an outspoken advocate for reform several years ago, when he discovered that, rather than risk dying on the U.S. wait list, many of his wealthier dialysis patients had their transplants done in China. There they could purchase the kidneys of executed prisoners. In India, Lawrence Cohen, another UC Berkeley anthropologist, found that women were being forced by their husbands to sell organs to foreign buyers in order to contribute to the family's income, or to provide for the dowry of a daughter. But while the WHO estimates that organ-trafficking networks are widespread and growing, it says that reliable data are almost impossible to come by. "Nancy has done truly courageous work, literally risking her life to expose these networks," says Delmonico. "But anecdotes are impossible to quantify."

Even as illegal trade is exposed, a roster of Web sites promising to match desperate dialysis patients with altruistic strangers continues to proliferate unchecked.

Scheper-Hughes acknowledges that in gathering these anecdotes she has frequently bumped up against the ethical boundaries of her own profession. While UC Berkeley (which funds most of her work) granted special permission for her to go undercover, she still takes heat from colleagues: misrepresenting oneself to research subjects violates a cardinal rule of academic research. "I expect my methods to be met with criticism," she says. "But being an anthropologist should not mean being a bystander to crimes against the vulnerable."

While Rosen has fared well since the surgery—he recovered quickly, used the money to travel and stays in touch with his kidney recipient via Facebook—most of the donors Scheper-Hughes and her colleagues have spoken with are not so lucky. Studies show that the health risks posed by donating a kidney are negligible, but those studies were all done in developed countries. "Recovery from surgery is much more difficult when you don't have clean water or decent food," says Scheper-Hughes. And research on the long-term effects of organ donation—in any country—is all but nonexistent.

The Declaration of Istanbul

Last May [2008], Scheper-Hughes once again found herself sitting across from a group of transplant surgeons. This time they were not as incredulous. More than 100 of them had come from around the world to Istanbul for a global conference on organ trafficking. Together, they wrote and signed the Declaration of Istanbul, an international agreement vowing to stop the commodification of human organs. But unless their document is followed by action, it will be no match for the thriving organ market. Even as illegal trade is exposed, a roster of Web sites promising to match desperate dialysis patients with altruistic strangers continues to proliferate unchecked. These sites have some surgeons worried. "We have no way to tell if money is changing hands or not," says Diflo. "People who need transplants end up trying to sell themselves to potential donors, saying, 'I have a nice family, I go to church,' etc. Is that really how we want to allocate organs?"

Maybe not. But in the United States, the average wait time for a kidney is expected to increase to 10 years by 2010. Most dialysis patients die in half that time, and the desperate don't always play by the rules.

9

Living Kidney Donations May Not Be Safe for Donors

R. Michael Hofmann

R. Michael Hofmann is an expert on kidney disease and a professor at the University of Wisconsin Medical School.

Although the short-term risks of kidney donation are well known and documented, little has been done to document the long-term health of kidney donors. Some studies indicate the donors develop hypertension at a higher than expected rate after they reach sixty years of age. In addition, some donors develop a condition called "proteinuria," marked by too much protein in the urine. This condition can lead to an increased risk of cardiovascular disease. Long-term studies of kidney donors must be undertaken to ascertain the risk to kidney donors over time.

More than 85,000 individuals are on the kidney transplant waiting list, according to the United Network for Organ Sharing (UNOS). Living kidney transplantation confers a survival benefit as well as a cost savings to the Medicare system. Although strategies for increasing the deceased donor pool—such as the use of kidneys donated after cardiac death and kidneys from expanded criteria donors[1] (ECDs)—have been modestly successful, they have still been unable to keep pace with the annual growth of eligible kidney transplant recipients. Therefore, the impetus for increasing sources of potential kidney donors has never been greater.

1. Donors who are older or have certain medical conditions that would have made them ineligible to donate kidneys in the past.

R. Michael Hofmann, "Living Kidney Donation: How Safe Is It?" *Renal and Urology News* vol. 9, no. 9, September 2010, pp. 17–19. Copyright © 2010 by Haymarket Media, Inc. All rights reserved. Reproduced by permission.

The first successful living kidney transplantation was performed between identical twins in Boston in 1954 by Joseph Murray, MD. At that time, it was considered experimental and highly controversial to be doing a kidney transplant for end-stage renal disease (ESRD), let alone putting the life of another individual at risk by removing a kidney with no medical benefit to the donor. Fifty-six years later, living kidney donation happens at transplant centers across the nation on a daily basis for those at ESRD who are lucky enough to have a living donor willing to share the gift of life with them.

But what do we really know about the safety of living kidney donation? The short term risks of surgical complications, including mortality and morbidity, are well defined and so informing the potential donor about his risk of dying, developing a wound infection, bleeding, chronic pain, and so forth are fairly well established. However, information about long-term risks is more nebulous. The dearth of safety data two, three, and four decades after kidney donation creates some uncertainty when obtaining informed consent from a young potential donor.

The Risk of Death After a Kidney Donation

Perioperative risk is characterized as any death within a defined period of time after surgical donation of a kidney. Studies have defined this period anywhere from 30 days up to 90 days after donation. The risk of death due to donation has been reported from 0 per 1,000 donations up to 3.1 per 100,000 donations. The study by [Dr. Dorry] Segev [and colleagues] was the largest study of donors to date and was therefore best powered to detect a difference in mortality as compared to most of the previous single-center studies. The study also noted an increased risk in males, blacks, and those with hypertension. It is interesting to note that the mortality rate did not increase despite the increasing age of the donors over the study period. In general, this is considered an acceptable rate of surgical death. This mortality rate is similar to that seen with laparoscopic cholecystectomy but with one tremendous difference: the living kidney donor receives no medical benefit.

The Long Term Risk of Death for Kidney Donors

Many single-center studies have found no increased risk of death in long-term living kidney donors, and some researchers have even suggested improved overall survival of kidney donors. But these studies have been hampered by small size, frequent patient loss to follow up, and lack of an adequate control group to adequately study this question. Standard mortality rates for the general population are often used as a control but these rates can potentially fail to adequately control for co-morbid diseases found in the general population. In one of the largest single-center studies of living donors, there did not appear to be an increased risk of death compared with the general population even up to 40 years after donation. However, the number of donors studied beyond 20 years after donation is limited, so it is difficult to draw long-term conclusions. This lack of long-term data has further bolstered the call for a unified national donor registry in the United States.

The Risk of Hypertension

The risk of developing hypertension (HTN) [abnormally high blood pressure] after living kidney donation is a complex issue. First, there are often subtle differences in what each center defines as HTN. Some centers have defined HTN as a systolic BP [blood pressure as the heart pumps; first number in blood pressure reading] greater than 130 mm Hg, whereas others have used a systolic BP greater than 140 mm Hg as their cut off. Also, there is a high rate of donors who display white coat HTN[2] at evaluation. Not surprisingly, the risk of developing HTN after living kidney donation has been evaluated in multiple studies with conflicting results. [Dr. Rajiv] Saran and colleagues noted that up to 75% of their donors had developed HTN, which was significantly above the rate predicted by data from the National Health and Nutritional Examination Survey. However, the number of donors—47—was small. It is well known that as a person ages the elasticity of the arteries decreases. This, combined with cardiovascular calcification, is felt to be at the root of age-related HTN. Whether there is an increased risk of HTN due to the decrease in renal mass following living kidney donation as suggested by [Dr. Bertram] Kasiske and colleagues remains unclear. This makes interpreting the normal age-related risk of HTN difficult to assess versus an increased risk due to living kidney donation. [Dr. Robert A.] Gossmann et al. found an increase in systolic pressures 11 years after living kidney donation. It is interesting to note that none of the donors were hypertensive prior to donation, but 30% were taking antihypertensive medications 11 years after donation. However, when comparing age-matched controls they noted that there was no significant difference in BP after living kidney donation. And when [other researchers] compared BP in living donors versus non-donor siblings—thus controlling for genetic susceptibility, they found no increased risk of hypertension after kidney donation.

However, in a meta-analysis of 5,145 living donors, [Prof. Neil] Boudville [and colleagues] found a 5 mm Hg increase in BP five to 10 years after living kidney donation. The researchers noted that a higher risk for developing hypertension occurred in donors older than 60 years, donors with higher pre-donation BP, African-American donors, and those with low pre-donation glomerular filtration rate (GFR) [a measure of

2. People with "white coat" hypertension generally have normal blood pressure that rises into hypertension when they are in the presence of doctors or medical staff (who usually wear white coats).

kidney function]. This seems like a relatively small increase in BP but it should be kept in mind that a 10 mm Hg increase in systolic pressure and a 5 mm Hg increase in diastolic pressure translate into a 1.5 fold increase risk of death from myocardial infarction [heart attack] and . . . stroke.

With the continued shortage of living donors, some centers have begun the practice of accepting certain donors who are hypertensive prior to kidney donation. Although short-term results demonstrate no adverse outcomes, it remains a group where long-term data are sorely needed.

Too Much Protein in the Urine

Proteinuria, specifically albuminuria,[3] is generally considered a marker of early renal disease. It often . . . is correlated with increased cardiovascular mortality risk. Whether this holds true for living kidney donors after donation is unclear. There is a suggestion that the proteinuria following living kidney donation may occur through a different mechanism than normally occurs in renal disease, suggesting the risk of developing progressive CKD [chronic kidney disease] is reduced. In either case, proteinuria has been noted as a long-term consequence of living kidney donation in 5%–56% of donors. In the study [led] by Gossmann, there was a particularly high rate of proteinuria after living kidney donation (56%) but the number of patients with albuminuria was much lower. This suggests that their method for detecting proteinuria was extremely sensitive, leading to an unusually high rate of proteinuria after kidney donation. Similar to studies assessing the risk of hypertension, most studies looking the proteinuria following living kidney donation were small single-center studies with many donors lost to follow up and relatively homogenous donor ethnicity, which limited the applicability of the findings to all populations. In a recent large study, [Dr. Hassan] Ibrahim [and col-

3. Conditions where there is an abnormally high level of protein in the urine. Albumin is a type of protein.

leagues] found that the risk of developing proteinuria increased with time after donation and in male donors. Their results demonstrated microalbuminuria in 11.5% of living donors; 1.2% had macroalbuminuria. A recent meta-analysis designed to assess the risk of proteinuria after living kidney donation determined the rate of proteinuria to be 12% at an average of seven years post donation. Therefore, it appears the true incidence is close to the findings of the two aforementioned studies. . . .

As physicians, we all take the Hippocratic oath and pledge to first and foremost cause no harm to our patients, but in [the case of kidney donors], do we really know?

The Risk of End Stage Renal Disease [ESRD]

The risk of developing ESRD after living kidney donation does not appear to be worse than the general population, supporting the notion that living kidney donation is safe. This is controversial, however. According to the current literature, the risk of developing ESRD after living kidney donation ranges from 0.1%–1.1%. Most studies, however, were not sufficiently powered to provide an accurate assessment of risk. The study by Ibrahim et al. found that the ESRD rate among living kidney donors was 180 per 1 million people, which compares favorably to the national rate of 268 per 1 million. However, individuals have to undergo rigorous screening to become donors, raising the question of whether the general population is an adequate control group for comparison.

Aging Donors and Changing Demographics

Although living kidney donation is considered relatively safe, long-term risks of living kidney donation remain unclear. Even more concerning is the slow shift in demographics of the average living donor. The average age of living donors has increased with time. In 1998, 13.9% of donors were aged 50 years or older compared with 22.8% in 2008. In addition, obesity within the donor population has also increased. In 2000, 17% of donors were obese; this percentage rose to 21% in 2007. In addition, some centers now accept select patients with hypertension for living kidney donation. In fact, in a recent review of kidney donors, up to 24% were found to be medically complex, which was defined as obese . . . , hypertensive, or having a [low] GFR. The increasing demand for living donors to fill the void between new potential kidney recipients and deceased kidney donors has caused more transplant centers to consider living donors with isolated medical abnormalities (IMA) as potential donors. These are people who would likely have been turned down as living donors one or two decades ago. However, long-term outcome data for donors with IMAs are lacking. Clearly, there is a critical need for better and larger studies reviewing long-term outcomes for living kidney donors. The creation of a national database to study outcomes of living kidney donors would be a large step forward in that direction. As physicians, we all take the Hippocratic oath and pledge to first and foremost cause no harm to our patients, but in this case, do we really know?

Key Points About Kidney Donor Safety

- The ESRD risk following living kidney donation does not appear to be worse than the general population.

- Studies examining the post-operative risk of hypertension have produced conflicting results.

- Data suggest that living kidney donation is not associated with an accelerated decline in GFR.

10

The Criteria for Determining Donor Death Should Be Changed

Robert D. Truog and Franklin G. Miller

Robert D. Truog is a professor of medical ethics and anesthesia in the Departments of Anesthesia and Social Medicine at Harvard Medical School and the Division of Critical Care Medicine at Children's Hospital in Boston. Franklin G. Miller is a faculty member in the Department of Bioethics at the National Institutes of Health in Bethesda, Maryland.

The dead donor rule is an ethical requirement that patients must be declared dead before organs can be removed for transplantation into other bodies. However, when patients are declared brain-dead, or declared dead on the basis of cardiac death, the patients are not truly dead under commonly understood definitions of death, but are considered dead solely for the requirement of the dead donor rule. Removing organs for transplantation from a patient who has no hope of recovery is ethical; the dead donor rule must be changed to reflect this.

Since its inception, organ transplantation has been guided by the overarching ethical requirement known as the dead donor rule, which simply states that patients must be declared dead before the removal of any vital organs for transplantation. Before the development of modern critical care, the diagnosis of death was relatively straightforward: patients were dead when they were cold, blue, and stiff. Unfortunately, organs from these traditional cadavers cannot be used for transplantation. Forty years ago, an ad hoc committee at Harvard Medical School, chaired by Henry Beecher, suggested revising the definition of death in a way that would make some patients with devastating neurologic injury suitable for organ transplantation under the dead donor rule.[1]

The concept of brain death has served us well and has been the ethical and legal justification for thousands of life-saving donations and transplantations. Even so, there have been persistent questions about whether patients with massive brain injury, apnea, and loss of brain-stem reflexes are really dead. After all, when the injury is entirely intracranial, these patients look very much alive: they are warm and pink; they digest and metabolize food, excrete waste, undergo sexual maturation, and can even reproduce. To a casual observer, they look just like patients who are receiving long-term artificial ventilation and are asleep.

Although it may be ethical to remove vital organs from ... patients, we believe that the reason it is ethical cannot convincingly be that the donors are dead.

The arguments about why these patients should be considered dead have never been fully convincing. The definition of brain death requires the complete absence of all functions of the entire brain, yet many of these patients retain essential neurologic function, such as the regulated secretion of hypothalamic hormones.[2] Some have argued that these patients are dead because they are permanently unconscious (which is true), but if this is the justification, then patients in a perma-

1. A definition of irreversible coma: report of the ad hoc committee of the Harvard Medical School to examine the definition of brain death. JAMA 1968;205:337–40.

2. Truog RD. Is it time to abandon brain death? Hastings Cent Rep 1997;27:29–37.

nent vegetative state, who breathe spontaneously, should also be diagnosed as dead, a characterization that most regard as implausible. Others have claimed that "brain-dead" patients are dead because their brain damage has led to the "permanent cessation of functioning of the organism as a whole."[3] Yet evidence shows that if these patients are supported beyond the acute phase of their illness (which is rarely done), they can survive for many years.[4] The uncomfortable conclusion to be drawn from this literature is that although it may be perfectly ethical to remove vital organs for transplantation from patients who satisfy the diagnostic criteria of brain death, the reason it is ethical cannot be that we are convinced they are really dead.

Over the past few years, our reliance on the dead donor rule has again been challenged, this time by the emergence of donation after cardiac death as a pathway for organ donation. Under protocols for this type of donation, patients who are not brain-dead but who are undergoing an orchestrated withdrawal of life support are monitored for the onset of cardiac arrest. In typical protocols, patients are pronounced dead 2 to 5 minutes after the onset of asystole (on the basis of cardiac criteria), and their organs are expeditiously removed for transplantation. Although everyone agrees that many patients could be resuscitated after an interval of 2 to 5 minutes, advocates of this approach to donation say that these patients can be regarded as dead because a decision has been made not to attempt resuscitation.

This understanding of death is problematic at several levels. The cardiac definition of death requires the irreversible cessation of cardiac function. Whereas the common understanding of "irreversible" is "impossible to reverse," in this

3. Bernat JL, Culver CM, Gert B. On the definition and criterion of death. Ann Intern Med 1981;94:389–94.

4. Shewmon DA. Chronic "brain death": meta-analysis and conceptual consequences. Neurology 1998;51:1538–45.-

context irreversibility is interpreted as the result of a choice not to reverse. This interpretation creates the paradox that the hearts of patients who have been declared dead on the basis of the irreversible loss of cardiac function have in fact been transplanted and have successfully functioned in the chest of another. Again, although it may be ethical to remove vital organs from these patients, we believe that the reason it is ethical cannot convincingly be that the donors are dead.

At the dawn of organ transplantation, the dead donor rule was accepted as an ethical premise that did not require reflection or justification, presumably because it appeared to be necessary as a safeguard against the unethical removal of vital organs from vulnerable patients. In retrospect, however, it appears that reliance on the dead donor rule has greater potential to undermine trust in the transplantation enterprise than to preserve it. At worst, this ongoing reliance suggests that the medical profession has been gerrymandering the definition of death to carefully conform with conditions that are most favorable for transplantation. At best, the rule has provided misleading ethical cover that cannot withstand careful scrutiny. A better approach to procuring vital organs while protecting vulnerable patients against abuse would be to emphasize the importance of obtaining valid informed consent for organ donation from patients or surrogates before the withdrawal of life-sustaining treatment in situations of devastating and irreversible neurologic injury.[5]

What has been the cost of our continued dependence on the dead donor rule? In addition to fostering conceptual confusion about the ethical requirements of organ donation, it has compromised the goals of transplantation for donors and recipients alike. By requiring organ donors to meet flawed definitions of death before organ procurement, we deny patients and their families the opportunity to donate organs if

5. Miller FG, Truog RD. Rethinking the ethics of vital organ donation. Hastings Cent Rep (in press).

the patients have devastating, irreversible neurologic injuries that do not meet the technical requirements of brain death. In the case of donation after cardiac death, the ischemia time inherent in the donation process necessarily diminishes the value of the transplants by reducing both the quantity and the quality of the organs that can be procured.

As an ethical requirement for organ donation, the dead donor rule has required unnecessary and unsupportable revisions of the definition of death.

Many will object that transplantation surgeons cannot legally or ethically remove vital organs from patients before death, since doing so will cause their death. However, if the critiques of the current methods of diagnosing death are correct, then such actions are already taking place on a routine basis. Moreover, in modern intensive care units, ethically justified decisions and actions of physicians are already the proximate cause of death for many patients—for instance, when mechanical ventilation is withdrawn. Whether death occurs as the result of ventilator withdrawal or organ procurement, the ethically relevant precondition is valid consent by the patient or surrogate. With such consent, there is no harm or wrong done in retrieving vital organs before death, provided that anesthesia is administered. With proper safeguards, no patient will die from vital organ donation who would not otherwise die as a result of the withdrawal of life support. Finally, surveys suggest that issues related to respect for valid consent and the degree of neurologic injury may be more important to the public than concerns about whether the patient is already dead at the time the organs are removed.

In sum, as an ethical requirement for organ donation, the dead donor rule has required unnecessary and unsupportable revisions of the definition of death. Characterizing the ethical requirements of organ donation in terms of valid informed consent under the limited conditions of devastating neuro-logic injury is ethically sound, optimally respects the desires of those who wish to donate organs, and has the potential to maximize the number and quality of organs available to those in need.

11

Brain Death Is an Ethical Criterion for Organ Removal for Transplantation

James M. Dubois

James M. Dubois is the Hubert Mäder Professor and department chair of health care ethics at Saint Louis University.

Although the Catholic Church is a long-time supporter of organ transplantation, some members are contesting brain death as adequate criteria for the determination of death. This is based on a misunderstanding of the facts and confusion between brain death and persistent vegetative state. It is possible that those who contest the brain death criteria are fundamentally opposed to all organ donations. However, Pope John Paul II stated that it is ethical for a trained health care worker to use neurological criteria to determine death, and it is ethical to transplant organs from such a patient.

Few medical procedures have proven to be as effective in saving lives as organ transplantation. Patients on the verge of death from organ failure often live a decade or longer after receiving a transplant. The Catholic Church, and the late Pope John Paul II in particular, have been enthusiastic proponents of this extraordinary medical procedure. According to the Catechism of the Catholic Church, "organ donation after death is a noble and meritorious act and is to be encouraged as an expression of generous solidarity". Yet despite the church's longstanding support for organ donation, some Catholic pro-life groups challenge practices essential to it.

The latest challenge pertains to so-called brain-death criteria, which are used to declare death in over 90 percent of all cases of organ donation in the United States. In a front-page article in *L'Osservatore Romano* (9/2/08), Lucetta Scaraffia, a professor of history at La Sapienza University in Rome and a frequent contributor to the Vatican newspaper, argued that the Catholic Church must revisit the question of brain death because it rests on an understanding of human life that is contrary to Catholic teaching. While Federico Lombardi, S.J., director of the Vatican press office, quickly stated that Scaraffia spoke for herself and not for the magisterium, her article shows there is disagreement within the church on the question of organ donation.

One really should not speak of 'brain death'—as if only the brain has died—but rather of the death of the human being, which may be determined neurologically.

Earlier this year [2009], Paul Byrne, M.D., a former president of the Catholic Medical Association and a long-time opponent of brain-death criteria, published a letter on the Web site *Renew America* arguing that God's law and the natural law preclude "the transplantation of unpaired vital organs, an act which causes the death of the 'donor' and violates the fifth commandment of the divine Decalogue, 'Thou shalt not kill' (Dt. 5:17)." The letter was signed by over 400 individuals, including at least three Catholic bishops and many pro-life program directors.

Organ Donation as an Act of love

In 1985 and 1989 the Pontifical Academy of Science studied the question of brain death and concluded that neurological criteria are the most appropriate criteria for determining the death of a human being. In the academy's view, one really should not speak of "brain death"—as if only the brain had died—but rather of the death of the human being, which maybe determined neurologically.

In 2000 Pope John Paul II expressed support for organ donation and the use of neurological criteria. He wrote: "The criterion adopted in more recent times for ascertaining the fact of death, namely the complete and irreversible cessation of all brain activity, if rigorously applied, does not seem to conflict with the essential elements of a sound anthropology." He concluded that "a health worker professionally responsible for ascertaining death can use these criteria. . . ." Moreover, he strongly reasserted his support for organ donation, calling it a "genuine act of love" and noting that he had earlier called it a "way of nurturing a genuine culture of life."

There is no documented case of a patient recovering from brain death.

To be fair, the Pontifical Academy of Science has no moral teaching authority, and a papal allocution is not the same as a papal encyclical or conciliar teaching. Still, it is ironic that many of the same people who continue to question brain-death criteria after John Paul II's allocution argue that the same pope's allocution on artificial nutrition and hydration for patients in a permanent vegetative state has decisively settled that matter.

For many people, concerns about brain death arise from a simple misunderstanding of the facts. I have spent years studying how the general public and health professionals understand death and organ donation. People in focus groups and surveys often confuse brain death with P.V.S. [persistent vegetative state] Yet P.V.S. patients breathe spontaneously and have sleep-wake cycles. Brain-dead bodies depend upon artificial ventilation; without it there would be no respiration and no heartbeat. Moreover, many think it is possible to recover from brain death, just as patients sometimes recover from deep coma. Yet there is no documented case of a patient recovering from brain death, despite some popular reports of misdiagnosed brain death. An organ that has been deprived of oxygen sufficiently long will die, and it is medically impossible to change dead brain cells to living brain cells. Finally, about half of Americans do not know that brain death criteria are used legally in all 50 states to pronounce patients dead. They are also used in nearly all Catholic hospitals in the United States.

Answering Three Objections to Brain Death as a Criteria

While these factual misunderstandings are common among the general public, they are not the source of the concerns expressed by Catholic pro-life groups. Their objections to brain-death criteria tend to be more philosophical. In a recent article in *The National Catholic Bioethics Quarterly*, I have tried to address some of these concerns. Here I will summarize three key points.

Human development. Lucetta Scaraffia and others have voiced concern that if we decide a human being is dead because he or she lacks a functioning brain, then we will deny that embryos are human until they form a brain. However, we are developmental creatures: in our earliest days of development in the uterus, we do not depend upon a brain to live. Yet as we grow, we come to depend upon a functioning brain; and when it dies, we die. To argue that support for brain death criteria calls into question the status of early human life is to misunderstand basic human biology.

The unity of the human being. According to some Catholic pro-life advocates, the brain death criteria accepted by the larger medical community rest on a "dualistic" view of the human being that assumes the human soul is radically distinct from the human body. They argue that if the soul is the life principle of the body and if an artificially maintained brain-dead body shows some signs of life, like a beating heart, then the soul must be present. Like many members of the Catholic medical community, I do not dispute the Catholic understanding of life and death; we take seriously the fact that the soul and its proper functions are intimately bound with the body. Yet a mature human body that is functionally decapitated is no longer a living human being.

Ken Iserson, M.D., a professor of emergency medicine at the University of Arizona, cites the Talmud when describing brain death: "The death throes of a decapitated man are not signs of life any more than is the twitching of a lizard's amputated tail." If one rejects the notion that a decapitated body is a dead body, then one is left with a conclusion repugnant to common sense and good metaphysics: a severed head and a decapitated body would both have to be considered living human beings if separately maintained alive (a view held by at least one opponent of brain death criteria). In fact, to be wholly consistent, one would need to hold that each is independently the same living human being that existed prior to the decapitation—a view that flatly contradicts the unity required to be human.

Strange case reports. Following brain death, most bodies spontaneously lose circulation within days, even when they are artificially ventilated and provided with aggressive critical care. But there have been exceptional case reports of prolonged "survival" of the ventilated body. These are not misdiagnoses. In some cases, the entire brain liquefies and extremities begin to turn black. Despite continued circulation, there is no room for speculation that such bodies are any more conscious than a corpse that has been buried, and the likelihood of recovery is the same. Professor Scaraffia has noted that there have also been cases of pregnant women who were pronounced brain dead; yet with artificial ventilation and aggressive support their bodies sustained pregnancies until viability. But the fact that many parts of the body may survive and function for a time is wholly compatible with death of the human being. This is precisely what makes organ transplantation possible. The human heart may beat outside of the human body in a bucket of ice, and may even be transplanted and made to function again inside another human being. That the placenta and womb may survive and function in a body maintained artificially is similarly amazing, but it does not indicate that the womb belongs to a living human being. Importantly, none of these cases present "new data" that became available only after John Paul II's allocution, and thus they do not merit a re-examination of church teaching. They are well known, even if strange and rare, phenomena.

Human Bodies, Not Objects

In the end, I think these philosophical disputes about brain death are actually motivated by a much deeper, more fundamental opposition to organ donation. This is illustrated by the resistance pro-life groups have offered to other kinds of organ donation, including donation after cardiac death. This opposition ultimately is driven by two deeper concerns that often go unarticulated.

The ethical question at hand is how we should deal with the risk of treating persons as objects or commodities.

First, organ donation risks treating human beings or their deceased bodies as "objects." In John Paul II's 2000 allocution on organ donation and brain death, he stated that "any procedure which tends to commercialize human organs or to consider them as items of exchange or trade must be considered morally unacceptable, because to use the body as an 'object' is to violate the dignity of the human person." He also noted that organ donation requires the informed consent of the patient or the patient's family. Yet the continual shortage of organs leads some policymakers to consider payments for organs and even organ procurement without expressed consent. Overly hasty pronouncements of brain death—which are rare but have received considerable attention in recent years—also reinforce suspicions that a concern for organ donation is trumping care for patients.

The ethical question at hand is how we should deal with the risk of treating persons as objects or commodities. It is worth recalling that Hans Jonas, one of the more famous opponents of brain-death criteria, also expressed deep reservations about medical research in general, which has yielded numerous treatments, vaccines and cures. Jonas feared that such research tends by its very nature to treat human subjects as "objects" or things. But the Catholic Church does not view medical research as intrinsically wrong for that reason; rather, it suggests how research may be conducted respectfully. It is the same with organ donation.

Determining death in the context of organ donation is challenging and will likely remain controversial for the simple reason that death must be determined quickly lest all transplantable organs die with the human being.

A second obstacle to organ donation within some Catholic circles rests on a misunderstanding of the so-called precautionary principle. This principle has been used in Catholic social teaching and basically urges caution in the face of uncertainty regarding grave risks of harm (for example, the possible harm from genetic modification). Paul Byrne, M.D., and colleagues seem to seek an absolute certainty that death has occurred, one marked by the destruction of all major organ systems. This is why Dr. Byrne opposes not only brain death, but also deceased-organ donation; by the time he would consider a body dead, no organs would be healthy enough to transplant. Yet this desire for absolute certainty conflicts with what Pope John Paul II wrote on the subject. He stated that "a health worker professionally responsible for ascertaining death can use these [neurological] criteria in each individual case as the basis for arriving at that degree of assurance in ethical judgment which moral teaching describes as 'moral certainty.'" He added that this "moral certainty is considered the necessary and sufficient basis for an ethically correct course of action."

Determining death in the context of organ donation is challenging and will likely remain controversial for the simple reason that death must be determined quickly lest all transplantable organs die with the human being. Nevertheless, the decision to reject organ donation in the name of precaution is not without cost. Patients in need of an organ transplant will die years earlier than necessary, and families who often find organ donation consoling will be bereft of the opportunity to find some meaning in their loss. We may not do evil that good may come of it, but neither should we bury our talents out of fear.

12

Brain Death Is Not an Ethical Criterion for Organ Removal for Transplant

Paul A. Byrne

Paul A. Byrne is a neonatologist at St. Charles Mercy Hospital in Oregon, Ohio.

Patients who have been declared brain dead for the purposes of organ transplants are not truly dead because there has not been complete cessation of all of the functions of the brain, including the brain stem. In reality, when organs are harvested from a brain dead patient, they are being taken from a living body. Organs from a body that is completely dead are not useful for transplantation. Therefore, a patient's right to live is violated by the declaration of brain death and doctors who harvest organs from a brain dead person are committing homicide.

We are bombarded with propaganda that encourages organ donation. For an organ to be suitable for transplantation it must be taken from a living person.

Recent reports in the literature include:

- Dr. KG Karakatsanis of Greece evaluated current clinical criteria and confirmatory tests for the diagnosis of "brain death" to determine if they satisfied the requirements for the irreversible cessation of all functions of the entire brain including the brain stem. He reviewed medical, philosophical and legal literature on the subject of "brain death." He presented four arguments:

1. Many clinically 'brain-dead' patients maintain residual vegetative functions that are mediated or coordinated by the brain or the brainstem.

2. It is impossible to test for any cerebral function by clinical bedside exam, because the tracts of passage to and from the cerebrum through the brainstem are destroyed or nonfunctional. Furthermore, since there are limitations of clinical assessment of internal awareness in patients who otherwise lack the motor function to show their awareness, the diagnosis of 'brain death' is based on an unproved hypothesis.

3. Many patients maintain several stereotyped movements (the so-called complex spinal cord responses and automatisms) which may originate in the brainstem.

4. Not one of the current confirmatory tests has the necessary positive predictive value for the reliable pronouncement of human death.

5. Conclusion: According to the above arguments, the assumption that all functions of the entire brain (or those of the brainstem) in 'brain-dead' patients have ceased, is invalidated.

- In the *New England Journal of Medicine* on 8-14-08 it was reported that infants who were not "brain dead" were pronounced dead after life support was discontinued. When there was no detected pulse for only 1.25 minutes, the heart was then excised for transplantation.

- Dr. David Greer reported in *Neurology* (Jan 2008) that many highly regarded hospitals in the U.S. routinely diagnose "brain death" without following the guidelines promulgated in 1995 by the American Academy of Neurology (AAN). Researchers at the Massachusetts General Hospital surveyed the top 50 neurology and neurosurgery departments nationwide; 82 percent responded. Results showed that "adherence to the AAN guidelines varied widely, leading to major differences in practice, which may have consequences for the determination of death and initiation of transplant procedures. Apnea testing[1] was omitted by 27 percent; still more distressing is that many fail to even check for spontaneous respirations.

While the apnea test can only cause a patient with a neurologic problem to get worse, it is commonly done without full and explicit consent. The test involves turning off the ventilator to determine if he can breathe on his own; and if he cannot, the result is suffocation of this living human being. The sole purpose of the apnea test is to determine that the patient cannot breathe on his own in order to declare him "brain dead." It is illogical to do this stressful, possibly lethal, apnea test on a patient who has just undergone severe head trauma. To turn off the ventilator for up to 10 minutes as part of the declaration of "brain death" risks further damage and even killing a comatose patient, who might otherwise survive and resume spontaneous breathing if treated properly.

Organs Are Being Taken from Living Bodies

"In plain, straight talk," writes Dr. Lawrence Huntoon, editor-in-chief of the *Journal of American Physicians and Surgeons*, "the survey indicates a high likelihood that some patients are being 'harvested' in some hospitals before they are dead! In hospitals with aggressive transplant programs (hospitals make a huge amount of money on transplant cases), making sure a

---

1. A test performed to establish brain death.

patient is dead before going to the 'harvesting suite' may be viewed as a minor technicality/impediment."

In the largest study in the literature known as the Collaborative Study 10% at autopsy had no pathology in the brain. Only 27% of patients on the ventilator for 1 week had a "respirator brain." From the beginning "brain death" was not based on data that was not sufficient and acceptable scientifically for destruction of the brain much less death of the person.

"Brain death" never was, and never will be true death.

Now more than ever, there is great push to kill for organs. It was reported in the news that Zack Dunlap from Oklahoma was declared dead, and a transplant team was ready to take his organs until that young man moved. Instead of a calling it a reflex (as I have been told is commonly done), the transplant team was sent away.

This young man did not have a destroyed brain. Nevertheless, Zack would have been truly dead had they excised his heart for transplantation. He could hear the doctors discuss his "brain death," but he could not move at that time to tell them he was alive.

Brain death never was, and never will be true death. This has been known by neurologists and organ transplanters since the beginning of the multi-billion industry. So if a declaration of "brain death" is not true death, but organs are taken legally in accord with "accepted medical standards," why not continue to make "acceptable" this less stringent criteria?

In the 10 years after the ad hoc Committee conjured up the Harvard Criteria, 30 more sets were reported by 1978. Every set became less stringent. Less strict sets were reported until eventually there came about a criterion that does not fulfill any of the "brain death" criteria. This is known as donation by cardiac death (DCD). Organs are obtained for transplantation by first getting a DNR [Do Not Resuscitate] order, then taking the patient off life support and waiting until the patient is without a pulse. In the past the waiting time was 10 minutes, then shortened to 5 minutes, then 4, then 2 and now, in the the waiting time is only 1.25 minutes until they cut out the baby's heart.

A Shameful Process

How shameful can it get? Shame on the medical field for knowing and not protecting these patients! Shame on the transplantation organizations for valuing money over an innocent injured person's life! Shame on the US government, other governments, and clergy for allowing and even encouraging extracting vital organs for transplantation and research! When will doctors informed of the truth stand for life instead of being political creeps?

No matter how generous one might want to be by donating his own self, or vital organs from someone else to save others, suicide or homicide to save another is not morally acceptable.

The transplant world no longer waits for "brain death." Now the goal is to get a DNR. Then they wait until the pulse stops for as short a time as 1.25 minutes. Organs obtained deceptively, yet legally, are called donation by brain death (DBD) and donation by cardiac death (DCD). It is the excision of vital organs that finalizes the death of the donor.

What is going to happen when it becomes better known that "brain death" was a hoax from the beginning? Do doctors and laymen not realize that destroying human life before its natural end is a heinous crime? Do they not realize that excision of an unpaired vital organ for transplantation or research is imposed death, also known as euthanasia? Have they not been reading the papers about all those "donors" about to be sacrificed who suddenly wake up minutes before their organs were going to be extracted?

No matter how generous one might want to be by donating his own self, or vital organs from someone else to save others, suicide or homicide to save another is not morally acceptable.

13

Cardiac Death Is a Controversial Criterion for Organ Removal for Transplant

Alister Browne

Alister Browne is a clinical professor and ethics theme director with the Faculty of Medicine at the University of British Columbia.

The Canadian Council for Donation and Transplantation (CCDT) issued recommendations for organ harvesting after cardiocirculatory death. The recommendations are controversial for several reasons. First, the guidelines do not ensure that the patient is dead. To be ethical, the CCDT should increase the time after the absence of a pulse to 20 minutes; or explain to families the difference between the way death is ordinarily understood and the way it is determined for organ donation. Second, since no one knows if the donor experiences distress, to be ethical, painkillers must be administered, something which is not included in the guidelines.

The practice of transplantation the world over is governed by the dead donor rule: non-paired vital organs can be retrieved only from patients who are dead. It is therefore important to have clear criteria for the determination of death. Most transplantable organs come from patients who are declared dead by neurologic criteria. These patients are called heart-beating donors; they have suffered a catastrophic brain injury, have been ventilated, and have had their vital functions maintained mechanically up to the point at which death is declared and then beyond, until their organs are retrieved. The donor pool can be expanded by permitting an alternative form of donation known as donation after cardiocirculatory death (DCD), or non-heart-beating organ transplantation. The donors in this case are patients for whom there is no hope of recovery but who are not dying because of a brain injury and hence will not suffer the neurologic death necessary for them to become heart-beating donors.

DCD has been an accepted medical practice internationally for 15 years but came to Canada only in 2006, when the Canadian Council for Donation and Transplantation (CCDT) published its national recommendations. Countries that permit DCD have had variable success in increasing the supply of transplantable organs. DCD of kidneys, the organ with which the CCDT recommends that Canadian centres begin their DCD programs, serves as a good example. In 2003, kidneys donated after cardiocirculatory death accounted for only 4% of the total kidneys transplanted in both Spain, which has the highest per capita rate of transplantation of any organs, and the United States, which has the highest total number of transplants. By contrast, in the Netherlands, which was then the world leader in DCD, kidneys donated after cardiocirculatory death accounted for 39% of the country's kidney transplants. The effect of introducing DCD into Canada is uncertain, but [researchers Christopher James] Doig and [Graeme] Rocker estimate that DCD "could contribute to an increase in the number of solid organs for transplantation including 20% or more to the supply of kidneys, and increasing the supply of other solid organs including liver, pancreas or pancreatic islet cells."

The CCDT recommends that, for the purposes of DCD, death be diagnosed after 5 minutes of continuously observed absence of pulse, blood pressure and respiration after life support has been discontinued. This recommendation of a 5-minute interval coincides with that of the Institute of Medicine and is commonly accepted in North America and the United Kingdom. However, it falls short of the time frame of "at least 10 minutes of proven lack of circulation to the brain" estimated for the determination of neurologic death in a report by the US President's Commission for the Study of Ethical Problems in Medicine and Biomedical and Behavioral Research. It is also not a universally accepted interval for DCD, and lies between alternatives that include a 75-second interval advocated by [Dr. Mark] Boucek and colleagues, a 2-minute interval used in Pittsburgh and at some other US and UK centres and a 10-minute interval used at still other US and UK centres and at St. Michael's Hospital in Toronto.

The condition that patients are in when they are diagnosed as dead by cardiocirculatory criteria does not fit any of the common understanding of the word "death."

In its guidelines, the CCDT aimed to "promote patient-care-based principles for providing the option of donation within a sound ethical framework and provide guidance to individual programs in developing parameters for safe practice in this field." We can measure the success of the CCDT in achieving this aim by considering two of the questions most often asked by families thinking about DCD: "Is my loved one really dead?" and "Will he or she feel any pain?" It is reasonable to suppose that any acceptable DCD program will either enable a health care professional to answer those questions with an unequivocal "Yes" in the first instance and "No" in the second or, if not, to give families the information they need to make an informed decision about donation. In this article, I will argue that a program that follows the recommendations of the CCDT will do neither of these things and hence will not satisfy ordinary consent requirements.

Dead Is Not Necessarily Dead

The CCDT guidelines assume that once patients or their families consent to organ retrieval at death and understand that death will be declared by cardiocirculatory criteria, they have consented to organ retrieval at death as determined by those criteria. There would be no problem with this assumption if the condition that patients are in when they are diagnosed as dead by cardiocirculatory criteria were recognized as death by ordinary persons, for then there would be a clear match between what patients or families believed they were consenting to and what they were actually being asked to agree to. However, the condition that patients are in when they are diagnosed as dead by cardiocirculatory criteria does not fit any of the common understandings of the word "death." Some people understand the word to refer to a permanent physical state of a patient, characterized by irreversible coma, the absence of spontaneous respiration and heartbeat, the impossibility of spontaneous recovery of these functions (auto-resuscitation) and the impossibility of restoration of these functions by others through artificial resuscitation. Others understand death to occur as soon as there is no longer any possibility of auto-resuscitation, even if artificial resuscitation could conceivably restore respiration and heartbeat. Still others understand death to require the permanent absence of spontaneous respiration and heartbeat and that these functions are not artificially supported. Death determined by the CCDT's criteria for cardiocirculatory death, however, is not consistent with any of these understandings.

The possibility of auto-resuscitation after a 5-minute interval of continuously observed absence of pulse, blood pressure and respiration after life support has been discontinued has never been definitively ruled out. In addition, we do not know precisely when successful artificial resuscitation is no longer possible. The Institute of Medicine claims that "existing empirical data cannot confirm or disprove a specific interval at which the cessation of cardiopulmonary function becomes irreversible." The CCDT comments in its guidelines that it was unable to identify in its literature review any evidence that either auto-resuscitation can occur or artificial resuscitation can succeed after the 5-minute interval. However, given the limited number of studies that have been published on these issues, this alleged absence of evidence does not show that those things are impossible and hence does not contradict the Institute of Medicine's view. Indeed, nothing in the CCDT's guidelines document contradicts this view. It is also not clear that evidence is in fact absent, as there are reports of the so-called Lazarus phenomenon, wherein spontaneous recovery is claimed to have occurred well after the 5-minute interval. Furthermore, even if future empirical investigations were to determine that there is no possibility of auto-resuscitation or successful artificial resuscitation after a 5-minute interval, this does not change the fact that we do not know this now.

Once we see that the ordinary sense of death differs from the CCDT's understanding of this state, we can also see that most patients or families who have consented to having death determined by cardiocirculatory criteria have not realized that this consent entails death being declared when the CCDT wants to declare it. The natural way for patients or families to understand an invitation to have death declared by cardiocirculatory criteria is to assume that they are being asked to consent to a special way of determining when death in the ordinary sense occurs, that is, to determine the presence of an irreversible state by cardiocirculatory instead of neurologic means. However, this is not the way the CCDT understands consent to have death determined by cardiocirculatory criteria. It takes it, rather, as consent to have death declared as soon as the cardiocirculatory criteria for its determination are satisfied, whatever state the patient may be in at that time, which in this case is to have death declared when the patient is not known to be in an irreversible state. It is plain, however, that unless patients or families are told that this is the consequence of their consent, the CCDT's assumption about what their consent means is not correct: in other words, consent by patients or families to death being declared by cardiocirculatory criteria does not mean that they have consented to death being declared as soon as the cardiocirculatory criteria for its determination are satisfied.

Because patients who are candidates for [donation after cardiocirculatory death] are not neurologically dead either before or shortly after they are declared dead. . . the possibility that they may experience distress cannot be ruled out.

Accordingly, if the CCDT is to provide guidelines for DCD that satisfy consent requirements, it must do one of two things. It must either recommend that the interval be increased from 5 minutes to at least 20 minutes, so that death determined by cardiocirculatory criteria coincides with death in the ordinary sense of the term (it is sometimes argued that this would not greatly reduce the number of usable organs), or it must recommend that health care professionals disclose that death determined by cardiocirculatory criteria differs from death as ordinarily understood and explain the difference. Undertaking the latter option would certainly complicate the recruitment of organ donors and may diminish the number of donors. We cannot be sure that fewer donated organs would be available for transplantation, as the public may respond positively to a fully transparent DCD program. Nonetheless, regardless of its effect on the number of donated organs, full transparency must be pursued because organ retrieval requires consent, and consent requires that patients and their families truly understand what they are consenting to. One might object that the information that health care professionals would have to give to patients or their families to fully explain death by cardiocirculatory criteria would be overly complicated. However, physicians provide complicated information to patients and families at times of grief in other situations where consent is required (e.g., when there is a question of terminating life-sustaining treatment), and it is not clear why seeking consent to DCD should proceed on different principles.

Donation After Cardiac Death May Cause Pain and Suffering

The second way in which the CCDT's recommendations fall short of meeting consent requirements relates to their silence concerning the possibility of pain and suffering. There is a significant possibility of distress to the patient during DCD. Controlled DCD (which occurs after the planned withdrawal of life-sustaining therapy) may involve interventions such as vessel cannulation before life-sustaining therapy is withdrawn and death is declared and it may involve post-mortem interventions such as in situ preservation. Uncontrolled DCD (which occurs after unanticipated cardiac arrest) may additionally involve chest compressions and mechanical ventilation both before and after consent for DCD is obtained and typically requires the withdrawal of life-sustaining treatment. We know that all of these interventions cause distress to conscious patients who are not taking palliative medications. Because patients who are candidates for DCD are not neurologically dead either before or shortly after they are declared dead by cardiocirculatory criteria, the possibility that they may experience distress cannot be ruled out in either the preparation for DCD or during organ retrieval.

Given this possibility of pain and suffering, there are three approaches that can be taken: (1) provide palliative medications when there are physical signs compatible with distress; (2) withhold all such medications on the ground that even if signs of distress are occurring, the patient does not have sufficient cognition to interpret any sensations as noxious; or (3) provide palliative medications prophylactically to prevent any possible distress. The CCDT does not recommend any one of these approaches in particular. Instead, it proposes that the management of the dying process, including procedures to withdraw life-sustaining treatment, sedation, analgesia and comfort care, should proceed according to the existing practices of individual intensive care units. This would be appropriate if the 3 approaches were equally acceptable. That, however, is not so.

It is fair to assume that if families perceived that their family member could suffer during organ harvesting, they would be less likely to consent to the procedure.

The distress protocol for DCD that is perhaps the most common is based on the first approach, in which medication is provided contingent on signs compatible with distress. The Pittsburgh protocol, for example, stipulates that "if narcotics and sedatives are administered, these drugs must be titrated to the patient's need for provision of comfort. The administration of clinically appropriate medications in appropriate doses to prevent discomfort is acceptable, with titration of medication predicated on signs compatible with distress." The problem with such protocols is that they do not guarantee that organ donors will not experience distress. To have a distress protocol at all is to grant that DCD may involve distress to the patient, and to medicate only on signs suggestive of distress is to expose patients to the possibility of experiencing it. However, if there is a possibility of distress (however slight or transitory) this must be disclosed, for it is surely information that anyone would want to have before agreeing to DCD. It is fair to assume that if families perceived that their family member could suffer during organ harvesting, they would be less likely to consent to the procedure.

The second approach is no more acceptable than the first. It is highly speculative to claim that patients declared dead by the CCDT's cardiocirculatory criteria are in such a debilitated condition that they would not be able to experience distress. It may be true that when such patients exhibit signs compatible with distress they feel nothing objectionable. However, no one can know this, and many health care professionals—all those who subscribe to protocols based on the first approach, for instances—do not think it is true. Thus, centres that adopt the first or second approach will be faced with the invidious alternatives of either disclosing the possibility of distress (and thereby deterring donation) or not disclosing that possibility (and thereby violating consent requirements).

Pain Medication Must Be Administered Before Organ Harvesting

If the first or second approach is used to address the possibility of pain and suffering, consent problems will still exist even if there is full disclosure at the time that consent is sought. Patients themselves can choose to run the risk of distress. However, in most cases consent for DCD will be sought from families, and it is not clear that a family can consent on behalf of a loved one to a procedure that might cause their loved one distress. It is not enough that *the family* thinks that running the risk is acceptable: they must have some reason to think that *their loved one* would be willing to run the risk. The decision about whether to grant consent would be straightforward for the family if their loved one had directly communicated their willingness to be exposed to distress to them. However, in the absence of that surely rare event it is not at all straightforward, because then the family must infer the loved one's willingness from something else and it is not clear what that could be. They cannot infer it from the loved one's desire to be an organ donor, for organ donation is usually believed to be a procedure that does not involve any distress and they cannot infer the desire to undergo a procedure that carries the risk of distress from the desire to undergo one that is not believed to carry such a risk. It is also not easy to identify anything else that would enable the family to confidently say that their loved one would want to undertake that risk.

The conclusion that must be reached is that any protocol that does not entirely eliminate the possibility of distress will raise seemingly insurmountable ethical problems whether or not that possibility is fully disclosed. This points us toward the third approach (the prophylactic provision of palliative medications to prevent pain) as the protocol of choice.

Organizations to Contact

The editors have compiled the following list of organizations concerned with the issues debated in this book. The descriptions are derived from materials provided by the organizations. All have publications or information available for interested readers. The list was compiled on the date of publication of the present volume; names; addresses, phone and fax numbers, and e-mail and Internet addresses may change. Be aware that many organizations take several weeks or longer to respond to inquiries, so allow as much time as possible.

The American Academy of Medical Ethics (AAME)
PO Box 451, Bristol, TN   37621
e-mail: main@ethicalhealthcare.org
website: www.ethicalhealthcare.org

The mission of the AAME is to advocate for the values that have underpinned western medical care. The organization does so by conducting conferences, writing articles, undertaking research, and teaching in the field of ethics, medicine, and science. Its website includes discussions and articles on current issues such as organ transplantation; beginning of life; cloning and stem cell research; patient care; end of life issues; and the medical profession.

Center for Bioethics
N504 Boynton, 410 Church St. SE, Minneapolis, MN   55455
(612) 624-9440 • fax: (612) 624-9108
e-mail: bioethx@umn.edu
website: www.ahc.umn.edu/bioethics

The Center for Bioethics at the University of Minnesota aims to advance and disseminate information concerning ethical issues in health care and the life sciences. Publications include the *Bioethics Examiner* and a series of bioethics overviews on specific issues. A helpful publication is the book-length *Ethics of Organ Transplantation*, available on the group's website.

The Coalition for Organ-Failure Solutions (COFS)
(330) 701-8399 • fax: (720) 293-0117
e-mail: cofs@cofs.org
website: www.cofs.org

COFS is a non-profit international health and human rights organization working against trafficking human organs and toward ending the exploitation of the poor as organ donors. Its activities include advocacy and support for survivors. The COFS website contains information about organ transplants and trafficking, and also includes the full text of the "People's Charter for Health." The site also includes videos of transplant trafficking victims telling their stories.

Children's Organ Transplant Association (COTA)
2501 West COTA Dr., Bloomington, IN   47403
(800) 366-2682 • fax: (812) 336-8885
e-mail: cota@cota.org
website: www.cota.org

The Children's Organ Transplant Association helps children and young adults who need organ transplants by providing fundraising help and family support. The organization's website includes information concerning the costs associated with transplants, news releases and information about transplants, and first-person accounts of transplant recipients.

The National Catholic Bioethics Center
6399 Drexel Rd., Philadelphia, PA   19151
(215) 877-2660 • fax: (215) 877-2688
e-mail: info@ncbcenter.org
website: www.ncbcenter.org

The National Catholic Bioethics Center conducts research and education to "promote human dignity in health care ... and derives its message directly from the teachings of the Catholic Church," according to the organization's website. The website includes the full text of the Vatican's *Dignitas Personae* instruction as well as bioethics FAQs. The organization also publishes a quarterly newsletter available online.

National Health Information Center
PO Box 1133, Washington, DC   20013-1133
(800) 336-4797
e-mail: healthfinder@nhic.org
website: www.healthfinder.gov

The National Health Information Center (NHIC) is a United States government organization devoted to providing reliable health information. The NHIC maintains the Healthfinder.gov website, a source that provide an extensive encyclopedia of over 1600 articles from trusted sources on health topics. In addition, the website also provides access to up-to-the-minute health news as well as offering tools for individuals to assess their own health.

National Institutes of Health (NIH)
9000 Rockville Pike, Baltimore, MD   20892
(301) 496-4000
e-mail: NIHinfo@od.nih.gov
website: www.nih.gov

The National Institutes of Health is the medical research agency of the United States. The NIH provides consumer health information as well as information about clinical trials on its website. In addition, the website features relevant news stories as well as both audio and video programming.

Office on Women's Health
US Department of Health and Human Services
Washington, DC   20201
(800) 994-9662
website: www.womenshealth.gov

The Office on Women's Health maintains the website *Womens Health.gov*. The website includes a wealth of information regarding women's health by topic, including a list of frequently asked questions regarding organ donation and transplantation. The site also offers publications such as a women's health calendar, posters, and brochures on girls' health as well as women's health.

United Network for Organ Sharing (UNOS)
PO Box 2484, Richmond, VA   23218
(804) 782-4800 • fax: (804) 782-4817
website: www.unos.org

United Network for Organ Sharing (UNOS) is the private, non-profit organization that manages the United States' organ transplant system under contract with the US government. They manage the national transplant waiting list and maintain a database that contains all organ transplant data for every transplant that occurs in the US. The organization also maintains educational materials on its website, including a history of organ transplantation, information on organ allocation, patient brochures and fact sheets, and a full library of research articles and statistics.

World Health Organization (WHO)
Avenue Appia 20, Geneva 27   1211
  Switzerland
+ 41-22-791-21-11 • fax: + 41-22-791-31-11
e-mail: info@who.int
website: www.who.int

The World Health Organization is the directing and coordinating authority for health of the United Nations. The WHO website includes multimedia presentations, fact sheets, news articles, publications, brochures and statistics. An essential starting place for any student of health-related issues, including organ transplants, the website also offers online books for download, and information on ordering materials through the mail.

Bibliography

Books

Norman L. Cantor — *After We Die: The Life and Times of the Human Cadaver*, Washington, DC: Georgetown University Press, 2010.

Annie Cheney — *Body Brokers: Inside America's Underground Trade in Human Remains*, New York: Broadway Books, 2006.

John Connell — *Medical Tourism*, Wallingford, UK: CABI, 2010.

Donna Dickenson — *Body Shopping: The Economy Fuelled by Flesh and Blood*, London: One World Publishing, 2008.

Anne-Maree Farrell, David Price, and Murieann Quigley, eds. — *Organ Shortage: Ethics, Law, and Pragmatism*, Cambridge: Cambridge University Press, 2011.

Michele Goodwin — *Black Markets: The Supply and Demand of Body Parts*, Cambridge: Cambridge University Press, 2006.

Kieran Healy — *Last Best Gifts: Altruism and the Market for Human Blood and Organs*, Chicago: University of Chicago Press, 2006.

Chris Klug, with   *To the Edge and Back: My Story from*
Steve Jackson   *Organ Transplant Survivor to Olympic*
                     Snowboarder, New York: Carroll &
                     Graf, 2004.

David Reisman   *Health Tourism: Social Welfare*
                     Through International Trade,
                     Cheltenham, UK: Edward Elgar,
                     2010.

Sally Satel   *When Altruism Isn't Enough: The*
                     Case for Compensating Kidney
                     Donors, Washington, DC: AEI Press,
                     2009.

Periodicals and Internet Sources

ABC News: Health "Physicians Must Treat 'Transplant
                     Tourists,'" January 30, 2010. www
                     .abcnews.go.com.

Mark Ammann   "Would Presuming Consent to Organ
                     Donation Gain Us Anything But
                     Trouble?" *Health Law Review* vol. 18,
                     no. 2, March 22, 2010.

Kimberly G.   "Organ Harvesting and Transplants:
Baskette and   Like Other Technologies, Medical
John M. Ritz   Technology Has Been Changing
                     Human Life," *Technology Teacher* vol.
                     69, no. 7, April 2010.

Owen Beattie,   "Ethical Issues in Resolving the
et. al.   Organ Shortage: The Views of Recent
                     Immigrants and Healthcare
                     Professionals," *Health Law Review*
                     vol. 18, no. 2, March 22, 2010.

Sarah Boseley   "New Europe: Spain's Family Bonds Lie at the Heart and Soul of Great Healthcare," *Guardian*, March 31, 2011.

Natsuko Fukue   "Transplants Set to Increase," *Japan Times*, November 12, 2010.

Denise Grady   "One Death Provides New Life for Many," *New York Times*, May 17, 2011.

Brandon Keim   "Bioethicists Save Organ Donation by Tweaking the Definition of Death," *Wired*, June 13, 2009. www.wired.com.

Marc Lacey   "Transplants Cut, Arizona Is Challenged by Survivors," *New York Times*, December 19, 2010.

James E. McFeeley   "Considerations in Developing a Policy for Organ Donation after Cardiac Death," *Critical Care Alert*, February 1, 2010.

Vivian Nereim   "Program Aims to Increase Minorities' Organ Donation," *Pittsburgh Post-Gazette*, August 2, 2010.

Barbara K. Pierscionek   "What Is Presumed When We Presume Consent?" *BioMed Central Medical Ethics* vol. 9, no. 8, April 25, 2008. www.biomedcentral.com.

Daniel Sayani   "Colorado Proposes 'Presumed
                     Consent' Organ Harvesting," *New
                     American*, January 24, 2011.
                     http://thenewamerican.com.

Rob Stein   "Infant Transplant Procedure Ignites
                     Debate," *Washington Post*, August 14,
                     2008.

Robert M. Veatch   "Donating Hearts after Cardiac
                     Death—Reversing the Irreversible,"
                     New England Journal of Medicine vol.
                     359, August 14, 2008.

Index

A

Academic research ethics, 69

Adolescents, 58–61

Age, 33–34, 55–57, 58–61, 77

Albuminuria, 75–76

Allocation. *See* Distribution policies

Altruism, 20, 68

American Medical Association, 41

Apnea test, 94

Artificial resuscitation, 101–102

Australia, 38

Auto-resuscitation, 101–102

B

Baily, Mary Ann, 9

Beard, T. Randolph, 18

Becker, Gary, 43

Beecher, Henry, 79

"Best practice" procurement policies, 19, 24–25

Black market, 30–31, 42–43, 62–69

Brain death criteria, 35, 40–41, 79–80, 84–91

Bramstedt, Katrina A., 46

Brazil, 65–66

Brokered transplants. *See* Black market

Browne, Alister, 98

Byrne, Paul A., 85, 90–91, 92

C

Cadaveric organs
 brain death criteria, 84–91, 98–99
 criteria for death, 40–41
 dead donor rule, ethics of, 78–83
 distress, donor, 104–107
 family refusal rates, 34–35
 financial incentives, 27–28
 history of transplant technology, 21
 kidneys, 71
 "no give, no take" policies, 44–45, 47–54
 organ donor cards, 23
 procurement policies, 22–27
 selling, 14–16

Canada, 99–100

Canadian Council for Donation and Transplantation, 99–101

Caplan, Arthur, 11, 56

Cardiac death criteria, 80–81, 93–97, 99–101

Carney, Gavin, 38

Catholic Church, 84–91

Children
 black market organs, 66
 LifeSharers, 50
 "no give, no take" policies, 52

Children's Hospital of Pittsburgh, 60

China, 31

Cohen, Lawrence, 68

Collaborative Study, 95

Compliance, 58, 60

Cooke, Alistair, 32

Corneas, 40, 42

Cost issues, 30, 38, 43, 71

Cyclosporine, 7, 21

D

Dead donor rule, 78–83

Death criteria. *See* Brain death criteria; Cardiac death criteria

Deaths while waiting, 29, 40, 46

Decision making process, 59–61

Declaration of Istanbul, 69–70

Delmonico, Frank, 65, 69

Department of State, U.S., 65

Developing countries, 66, 68

Di Carlo, Antonio, 57

Dialysis, 34, 38, 43, 55, 70

Dialysis and Transplant Patients Association (Datpa), 43

Diflo, Tom, 67–68, 70

Directed donation, 49–51

Distress, donor, 104–107

Distribution policies

age, 33–34, 55–57

"no give, no take" policies, 44–45, 47–54

variation in, 12–14

Do Not Resuscitate orders, 96–97

Donors, standards for, 11–13, 41–42

Dualistic view of the human being, 87–88

Dubois, James M., 84

Duke University Medical Center, 59, 61

Dunlap, Zack, 95

E

The Economist, 29

Education programs, 8, 22–23, 47

Efficacy

age considerations, 55–57

vs. urgency, 13–14

Elias, Julio, 43

Ethics

academic research, 69

age of recipients, 55–57

brain death criteria, 84–91, 92–97

dead donor rule, 78–83

informed consent, 100–107

"no give, no take" policies, 44–45, 48

organ distribution criteria, 12–14

presumed consent, 17

selling organs, 14–16

Europe, 8, 16–17, 42

Eurotransplant, 48

F

Fairness. *See* Ethics

Families

donation of relatives' organs, 8

informed consent, 100–107

kidney donation, 20

kidney exchanges, 25

"no give, no take" policies, 45

refusal rates, 34–35

required referral policies, 24

required request policies, 23–24

Fifth Amendment, 17

Financial incentives

cadaveric organs, 27–28

Iran, 36–37, 43
public opinion, 53
See also Noncash incentives
Follow-up care, 58, 59, 61
Foreign recipients, 33, 51
Foy-Watson, Shani, 60, 61
Free riders. *See* "No give, no take"
policies
Functional years, 55–57
Funeral homes, 32

G

Greer, David, 93–94

H

Hakim, Nadey, 38
Harvard Criteria, 95
Health insurance, 38
Hearts, 17, 58–61
Hippen, Benjamin, 38
Hippocratic Oath, 15–16
History
first successful organ trans-
plant, 7
kidney transplantation, 72
transplant technology, 19–22
Hofmann, R. Michael, 71
Hospitals, 23–24
Human development, 87
Human eggs market, 16
Huntoon, Lawrence, 94–95
Hypertension, 73–75

I

Immunosuppressive drugs, 7,
20–21
Incompetent adults, 52

India, 30–31, 42, 68
Infants, 93
Informed consent
cardiac death criteria, 100–107
John Paul II, Pope, 89–90
life support, withdrawal of,
81–83
Institute of Medicine, 100
Insurance, 38, 44
Interlandi, Jeneen, 62
International agreements, 69–70
Iran, 36–37, 43
Iserson, Ken, 88
Isolation, 59
Israel, 38, 45
Istanbul, 66, 69–70

J

Jackson, Jon D., 18
Jaquiss, Robert, 59
Jarvis, Rupert, 47
John Paul II, Pope, 84, 86, 89–91
Jonas, Hans, 90
Journal of the American Medical
Association, 41
Justice. *See* Ethics

K

Kaarakatsanis, K. B., 92
Kaserman, David L., 18
Kaufelt, Jonathan, 47
Kidnapped children, 66
Kidneys
black market, 30–31, 62–69
cardiac death criteria, 99
costs of kidney transplantation, 30
deaths while waiting, 40

CPSIA information can be obtained
at www.ICGtesting.com
Printed in the USA
FFOW04n0542230114
3237FF